MW00811496

THE HOARDING IMPULSE

There has been an increased awareness of hoarding in recent years, but clinical treatments aimed at helping people with this condition often have low success rates. In *The Hoarding Impulse* Renee M. Winters explores how depth psychology can enrich current conceptual models and treatment standards for compulsive hoarding. The book presents case studies of prominent sufferers including Edie and Edith Beale, the Collyer Brothers, and Andy Warhol and explores common themes of loss, shame and object clusters.

Winters sets out to provide a clear understanding of a hoarder's lived experiences and their core schemas of value, worth and personal identity, revealing a direct connection to excessive acquisition of objects. She illuminates the process of how objects can come to possess a hoarder and become not only their main source of happiness but also part of their identity and in doing so puts forward a new treatment plan based on providing a deeper understanding of and potent treatment approach to what is a core issue for hoarding individuals: the wounding of the soul. This new perspective to treating individuals who hoard helps them in the long term understand their processes, value system, and struggles with negative interpersonal relationships.

Providing a fascinating insight into the psyche of people who struggle with hoarding, this book will be essential reading for depth psychologists, Jungian psychotherapists, psychiatrists, social workers, students of analytical psychology and anyone interested in understanding the dynamics of this complex condition.

Renee M. Winters is a psychotherapist in private practice in California, USA., where she focuses on helping clients discover symbolic meaning and unconscious processing in their lives. Winters is a graduate of Pacifica Graduate Institute in Carpinteria, California where she earned her Doctorate in Philosophy in Depth Psychology with an emphasis in Depth Psychotherapy.

THE HOARDING IMPULSE

Suffocation of the Soul

Renee M. Winters

Routledge
Taylor & Francis Group

LONDON AND NEW YORK

First published 2015
by Routledge
27 Church Road, Hove, East Sussex, BN3 2FA

and by Routledge
711 Third Avenue, New York, NY 10017

Routledge is an imprint of the Taylor & Francis Group, an informa business

© 2015 Renee Winters

The right of Renee Winters to be identified as author of this work
has been asserted by her in accordance with sections 77 and 78 of
the Copyright, Designs and Patents Act 1988.

All rights reserved. No part of this book may be reprinted or
reproduced or utilised in any form or by any electronic, mechanical,
or other means, now known or hereafter invented, including photocopying
and recording, or in any information storage or retrieval system,
without permission in writing from the publishers.

Trademark notice: Product or corporate names may be trademarks
or registered trademarks, and are used only for identification
and explanation without intent to infringe.

British Library Cataloguing in Publication Data
A catalogue record for this book is available from the British Library

Library of Congress Cataloging in Publication Data
Winters, Renee M., author.
   The hoarding impulse: suffocation of the soul/Renee M. Winters.
   p. cm.
   Includes bibliographical references.
   I. Title.
   [DNLM: 1. Obsessive Hoarding – psychology. 2. Obsessive Hoarding –
   therapy. WM 176]
   RC569.5.H63
   616.85′84 – dc23
   2014048792

ISBN: 978-1-138-83900-7 (hbk)
ISBN: 978-1-138-83901-4 (pbk)
ISBN: 978-1-315-73065-3 (ebk)

Typeset in Bembo and Stone Sans
by Florence Production Ltd, Stoodleigh, Devon, UK

To Joanne C.

A woman whose beautiful soul helped illuminate this journey for me through the sharing of her pain and eventual triumphs. Your strength is inspiring.

CONTENTS

ACKNOWLEDGEMENTS

Quotes from *Grey Gardens* 2009, Home Box Office, Inc., all rights reserved, used with permission.

Quotes from *American Pickers* courtesy of History Channel.

Quotes from *Ghosty Men* © 2003, Franz Lidz, used with permission of Bloomsbury Publishing, Inc.

INTRODUCTION

Boxes to the ceiling, picture frames depicting past smiles, a hope chest containing old baby clothes, two old dressers full of children's artwork, and through the clutter in the corner, a small area long ago used for the practice of meditation. This woman's psyche speaks through her recounting of loss, abandonment, isolation, children she didn't have, a marriage that never happened, and a current life in which she felt stuck. She sat in despair, sad and tearful. Anxiety and embarrassment were present in the therapy room. She struggled to make sense of a life of which she was not proud.

As her therapist I have worked with this patient for numerous years, and through our encounter together arose an increased awareness of how her physical clutter seemed to tell a story about her psychological clutter or even provide her comfort as the psychological Other as well. As I began to formulate the premise of this book, I saw similarities to the psychological clutter that I have held onto over the last decade and how this contributed to my relationships with objects I possessed. With my clutter, I am safe. The clutter serves as a buffer, a safe zone packed with matter that keeps me from living outwardly. But could my need for safety interfere with psychological growth and ultimately become a denial of my wholeness? A journey had begun to find a deeper understanding to the questions that cluttered my conscious thoughts. I began researching this topic, meeting with individuals who suffered from hoarding tendencies, and a larger sense of purpose to uncover the hidden meaning behind obsessive acquiring began to form. Additional questions started to accumulate in my mind, like objects packed tightly into a hoarder's living room, multiplying over time spent with the topic. Could clutter have kept these hoarders closed off from an intimate and direct connection with life, family, friends, and companions? Was it done intentionally or from a place of unknowing; unaware of clutter's purpose? Was this due to dread of emotional chaos, or loss of control associated with a deep connection with others and themselves?

Our choices are often guided by the need for an integration of lifelong experience. It was no mistake that embarking on this book allowed a further unfolding of a personal and professional journey and a discovery of the true symbolic nature of my acquired clutter and that of other's who I accompanied during this journey. Synchronistically, I have had opportunities to work with numerous patients over the last year that suffer from their own forms of physical clutter. Like me, they are willing to journey into the underworld of the hoarder, embrace their shadow material, and emerge more conscious of self and psyche. By no mistake, a therapeutic encounter was created with these patients that allowed them, as well as myself, movement towards uncovering self and psyche that was embedded and hidden in the clutter.

> Jung considered that a neurosis is not only a defense against the wounding of life, but an unconscious effort to heal such wounds. Thus one may respect the intent of the neurosis if not its consequences. Symptoms, then, are expressions of a desire for healing.
>
> (Hollis, 1996, p. 10)

One of many definitions of compulsive hoarding is provided by the television program *Hoarders:* it is described for viewers watching the program as "a mental disorder marked by an obsessive need to acquire and keep things, even if the items are worthless, hazardous, or unsanitary." But from whose point of view are one person's objects seen as worthless? In the few years since this show was initially televised, there has been a shift away from objective judgment about the worth of possessions in definitions of this disorder. This signifies the importance of understanding value through the eyes of the hoarder. Depth psychology offers this essential exploration into the idiosyncratic meaning and value of objects to the person who possesses them. This book shows how depth psychology enriches current conceptual models and treatment standards for compulsive hoarding by providing a deeper understanding of and potent treatment approach to what could be a core issue for hoarding individuals, a crisis of the soul.

"It was in 1966 when Bolman and Katz used the term for the first time to describe a psychopathological phenomenon in an anecdotic case report" (Maier, 2004, p. 323), but the term *hoarding* has become increasingly common in psychiatric literature over the past decade. Additionally, the condition of hoarding has been gaining public notoriety over the last few years due to popular television programs such as *Hoarders* that depict their so-called natural settings—natural from the standpoint that they identify their cluttered, unliveable settings as "home" even after they have been deemed uninhabitable according to city regulations. The escalating public awareness of and interest in hoarding stories highlights the need for empirical study of this topic (Tolin, Meunier, Frost, & Steketee, 2010, p. 829). We must face the challenge to reach people who have hidden their disorder from the world due to their social isolation, shame, and limited insight and who rarely avail themselves of therapeutic intervention and testing.

People's increased knowledge and awareness of this often-obscure disorder can reduce stigmatization and encourage openness to research and intervention. In their comprehensive review of research, Mataix-Cols et al. (2010) concluded that "there is sufficient evidence to recommend the creation of a new disorder, provisionally called hoarding disorder" (p. 556) and, along with Pertusa et al. (2010), supported that, for most people, hoarding does not result from Obsessive-Compulsive Disorder (OCD) and is not just a symptom of Obsessive-Compulsive Personality Disorder (OCPD) (p. 383). Unlike OCPD, hoarding for most people is not a compulsive response to fear-provoking obsessions. Even though hoarding was listed as a symptom of OCPD in the *Diagnostic and Statistical Manual of Mental Disorders-IV* (American Psychiatric Association, 1994), many people who hoard do not possess this personality disorder.

Although hoarding can be a consequence of several other disorders, for most people it is a unique cluster of behaviors and etiologies that warrants its own diagnosis. Hoarding Disorder (HD) is included in the chapter "Obsessive-Compulsive and Related Disorders" in the DSM-5, and is characterized by a "persistent difficulty discarding or parting with possessions, regardless of their actual value . . . due to a perceived need to save items and to distress associated with discarding them" (American Psychiatric Association, 2013, p. 247). This results in living spaces being congested and cluttered with objects, making them unavailable for usual functions. Hoarding causes significant distress or impairment in several domains of human functioning. Over the years, enhanced clarification of the defining characteristics of hoarding has allowed better measurement of its prevalence, which is 2–5 percent of the U.S. population, likely double that of Obsessive Compulsive Disorder (Tolin et al., 2010, p. 829).

Increased knowledge and awareness of HD can reduce stigmatization and encourage openness to research and intervention. Frost and Steketee (2010) stated that an increasing amount of research on hoarding reveals that hoarders have an atypical emotional attachment to the inanimate objects that they accumulate, and they report high levels of anxiety: "If clutter prevents the person from using his or her living space and if acquiring and saving cause substantial distress or interference in everyday living, the hoarding is pathological. But exactly what kind of pathology is not clear" (p. 12). Perhaps the symbols of pathology lie with the hoarded objects themselves, allowing them to reach a symbolic level for the person. There is abundant literature on the disorder, but it is all written from a clinical or psychiatric point of view. Mataix Cols et al. (2010) stated that "hoarding as a characterological trait has its origins more than a century ago in the psychoanalytical concept of the 'anal character', which later became today's OCPD" (p. 557). Yet, as Joseph Cambray (2009) sensibly observes, "the best of analytic ideas need to be re-examined at least every generation to stay relevant, so they remain living ideas" (p. 2).

James Hillman (1981) beautifully articulated the shift away from psychology into a depth approach in his book *The Thought of the Heart and the Soul of the World*:

> Moving as well the seat of the soul from brain to heart and the method of
> psychology from cognitive understanding to aesthetic sensitivity . . . when
> the brain is considered to be the seat of consciousness we search for literal
> locations, whereas we cannot take the heart with the same physiological
> literalism.
>
> (p. 109)

Hoarders are literalists in Hillman's sense: they search for a literal location to
store the meaning of their lives, their sense of identity, nestled around them and
protecting them from what they consider to be a threat. Objects are a way for
them to enlarge their identity, to create a story of their life, perhaps as a way to
create meaning for a life not lived outside the dwelling.

As of today, there is no current literature on the condition of hoarding from a
depth psychological perspective. Therefore, the aim of this book is to provide a
synopsis of the current literature from a depth angle and explore how psyche and
self make themselves known in the images of a hoarder's setting and the objects
hoarders acquire, increasing consciousness from embracing painful revelations that,
when avoided, contribute to the pathology of hoarding. Additionally, this book
will help provide insight into why the depth perspective has been overlooked when
researching this compulsive behavior and what psyche and self have to tell us in
relation to one's setting.

According to Monika Wikman (2004), "the road to embodying hunger for
contact with the divine may be dominated initially by suffering and by explorations
in woundedness—such as becoming lost in complexes, addictions, or other painful
patterns that do not directly serve life" (p. 28). Projecting our shadow material
onto someone or something else is how we attempt to avoid our dark sides. Robert
Johnson (1991), in *Owning Your Own Shadow*, echoes what Monika Wikman stated
above: "To refuse the dark side of one's nature is to store up or accumulate the
darkness; this is later expressed as a black mood [depression], psychosomatic illness,
or unconsciously inspired accidents" (p. 26). When an individual who hoards denies
the existence of a problem and doesn't acknowledge his or her black mood, it is
difficult for deep emotions to surface, which is necessary to expand consciousness
and bring forth revelations.

Deviation from our normal ways, lacking an understanding of what is going
on, and not being understood by others keep us from setting things right. These
problems can blind hoarders to what and where things are going wrong in their
lives. Every individual who hoards is unique; their souls illuminate their peculiar-
ity through anxieties, compulsions, illusions, depressions, and overvalued ideas.
"Perhaps our psychopathology has an intimate connection with our individuality, so that our fear of being what we really are is partly because we fear the
psychopathological aspect of individuality" (Hillman, 1975, p. 55). From a societal
perspective, individuality is a double-edged sword, both encouraged and frowned
upon if we don't fit into a certain normalized ideal. Perhaps hoarding isn't about
how much stuff a person acquires due to their mental illness, but rather about how

one views the objects on a conscious level that doesn't fit a societal norm and therefore is repressed in the unconscious. In *On the Nature of the Psyche*, Carl Jung (1946/1960) postulated that "the more unconscious a man is, the more he will conform to the general canon of psychic behavior" (pp. 70–71), but the more conscious he becomes, the more he will live his individuality. Through expanding consciousness, can an individual who hoards live this second part Jung describes? By exploring our own minds with compassion and honesty, I believe we can face the pain in our lives and the problems of the world.

Distress that is directly related to hoarding behavior occurs when individuals have some insight and are able to see that the hoarding is not normal, but they can't seem to change it. Their embarrassment, shame, and fear reflect an awareness of their aberrant way of getting control through the out-of-control hoarding behavior. They fear social consequences, such as judgment and rejection, when people discover the hoard. Is there a connection between the internal process of the individual and the archetypal energy stored in the material that is hoarded? If there is a connection, then the goal would be to allow people who hoard to bring their unconscious conflict to consciousness so they can deal with the shadow material creatively instead of allowing it to be repressed into repetitive behaviors such as acquiring clutter—to allow processing of an object without judgment and with a welcoming sense of wonder to allow it to be what it is, as it is. The predicament that hoarders find themselves in with excessive acquisition is an abundance of chaos, both physically and emotionally, creating anxious energy within the body and mind. Marion Woodman further postulates, "Instead of holding the still point until the energy has a chance to transform into the ultraviolet side of the archetype [the contents of the collective unconscious], [hoarders] plunge into the infrared [illness]" (Woodman & Dickson, 1996, p. 189). The anxiety of facing life is primarily avoided, and when objects are removed, hoarders feel more vulnerable (expressed in grief, fear, and rage). The chaos of a life defined by avoidance of these feelings through hoarding encroaches on the health of physical and psychological systems, by preventing healthy and adaptable growth and change. Hoarders are like fugitives from life, even when the escape behavior is pleasurable. A person struggling with hoarding tendencies can be empowered by concentrating on an image and embracing their anxious energy to the point of allowing their rational mind no longer to experience fear and distress. Creating space for inquiry and providing guidance and reassurance can allow a person to feel supported in their efforts to understand the desire possessing them by an object.

Most people who hoard are excessive acquirers of objects. By acquiring, they could be seeking a comforting (ideological) attachment, seeking pleasure to avoid pain of unconscious material or pain associated with trauma or loss (neuroses), or simply seeking the stimulation from exploring and discovering their objects. The complexes that possess a patient are experienced daily and in their dreams, causing the ego to feel equally powerless and the patient to be emotionally out of control. The ego is fragile and hyperdefensive and fragments easily under stress. Stein (1998) states, "The stimulus that provokes the complex may be slight or great, of long or short duration, but its effects on the psyche can continue for extended periods of time and can come into consciousness in waves of emotions or anxieties" (p. 50).

The ego will attempt to protect the psyche from possible injury and intrusion by implementing defenses that keep the person walled off from the world. Perceiving their environment as overwhelming, individuals who hoard isolate themselves through excessive consumption of objects, walling off the world and creating a cocoon of safety that allows them to live in defensive isolation. In the book *Stuff*, Frost and Steketee (2010) provide an example of this type of living condition: "Getting from place to place required skating on top of the debris, and my feet were too big to avoid stepping on soda cans, vitamin bottles, or phone books" (p. 153). Left untreated, complexes endure through time and can be seen through a person's repetitive emotional reactions and discharges, errors in judgment and decisions, and lack of insight. The feelings of safety, identity, and opportunity hoarders receive from their objects are the catalyst in their attempts to avoid their psychic pain and all negative emotional experiences associated with collecting and discarding (Frost & Steketee, 2010, p. 154).

Much of the mainstream research on the topic of hoarding seems to want to cognitively understand and fix the patients' compulsion to hoard (in some sense not allowing the process to be "unfixed" or organic), ridding them of their distresses by medication and conventional interventions. However, many complexes that possess a patient cannot be forced to answer to the ego; they are obstinate to conventional clinical treatments, like pharmaceutical and traditional behavioral approaches. Progress through increased consciousness of core anxiety, fear, loss, and conflict that occurs by focusing on a single object might generalize quickly to other objects and decrease the need to avoid discomfort through hoarding. James Hollis (1998) echoed this statement in his book *The Eden Project*: "the treatment of soul is what heals" (p. 113). There is much to be gained from a depth psychological study of hoarding. One of the essential tenets of depth psychology is that psyche is more powerful than the force of the conscious mind, and the will and reason of conscious thought are overpowered by the influence of the unconscious (Jung, 1946/1960, p. 95). In considering hoarding behaviors (excessive acquisition of objects and ideological attachments) from a depth perspective, one is compelled to ask, "What does soul want in this cluttered and murky setting?"

The lack of research on hoarding from a depth psychological perspective is because depth psychology provides no tangible results that can be measured. However, clinical studies conducted on the condition of hoarding have been accomplished through ego-based work of strengthening brain function, problem finding and solving, mental inventiveness, and explanatory skill. Clinical psychology produced a fixed set of ideas and remedies that were duplicated to fit all people who hoard. Therefore, this book will induce reflection and insight and describe the personal descent into the underworld (deep suffering) of a patient who struggles to make conscious what lies stored in their setting. While exploring the underworld of a patient, the process of making conscious their shadow material can begin. Allowing openness to explore one's suffering is risky to a hoarder because it means venturing into unfamiliar ground, where the shadow lives and grows. Fear and vulnerability keep people from exploring their suffering, and therefore render them helpless to manage their relationship with objects.

Johnson (1991) has an insightful quote that resonates with this idea: "The shadow gone autonomous is a terrible monster in our psychic house" (p. 5). When people ignore the knocking at their psychic door from their shadow material wanting to make its presence known, the shadow grows into something more prominent, demanding attention. Acknowledging one's own shadow and incorporating it into one's understanding of self is unpleasant and therefore avoided. People tend to avoid unpleasant feelings, seeking relief through artificial joy and pleasure. So when their shadow material remains hidden, or repressed, it takes on a life of its own and will be displayed through neurotic behaviors. Jung's own sense, from his notes in the seminars of 1928–1930, was that "your brother, your shadow, [is] the imperfect being in you that follows after and does everything which you are loath to do, all the things you are too cowardly or too decent to do" (p. 76). One of life's great psychological tasks is the ability to honestly acknowledge and deal with one's own shadow material. Exploring the dynamics of people who hoard, focusing on the activity of the unconscious as the primary data for examination to help uncover core schemas of value, worth, and personal identity through acquisition that keeps these patients stuck in a debilitating situation is detailed in the pages that follow.

Illuminating and shifting the energy and affect of a person's hoarding behaviors into a different level of consciousness and understanding, allowing what the person hoards to speak for what hoarding means to them is the tenant of this book. By exploring this disorder, the reader is able to re-imagine the crisis of compulsive hoarding—a personal crisis of chaos that facilitates extreme isolation and excessive acquisition and ideological attachments, rooted in a setting where normal and abnormal cohabitate. Allowing for archetypal energies, synchronicities, and the imaginal by contextualizing the setting and objects possessed through a depth psychological lens allows a fresh approach to the clinical psychological literature that defines the hoarding epidemic currently. By reimagining the psychopathological and clinical spectrum of hoarding from a depth psychological perspective, the hope is that it will contribute to a broadening of its classification as a mental illness, yielding new treatment options with higher rates of successful intervention and a deeper understanding of why individuals suffer from this disorder.

1

HOARDING AS AN EPIDEMIC

The basic intention of this chapter is to use a depth psychological perspective to analyze the existing literature that explores compulsive hoarding activities. It allows the disorder to be explored for its disorder within an individual's life; namely, a form of disordered living in the disorder. That is the pathos for a hoarder: living in disorder in a literal way. Particular attention is being paid to both established and new literature regarding the phenomenon of the shadow and complexes as the pivotal turning points in understanding hoarding behaviors from a different theoretical viewpoint. Compulsive hoarding has received little empirical study compared to OCD and its ostensible subtypes. Pertusa *et al.* (2008) conclude in their summary of research that compulsive hoarding appears to be a syndrome that is separate from OCD in most cases and that is associated with substantial levels of disability and social isolation (p. 1296). This and other research led to the inclusion of Hoarding Disorder in the DSM-5 (American Psychiatric Association, 2013). This official recognition invites a deeper understanding of internal functions of hoarding people's lives, along with a refinement of assessment and intervention methods that reflect this understanding.

Contrary to clinical research, hoarding behaviors can be referenced as far back as the fourteenth century; Dante reserved the fourth circle of hell for hoarders and wasters in his *Inferno (Canto VII)*. Additionally, the character Krook, created by Charles Dickens in *Bleak House,* was described as "possessed of documents" in a shop where "everything seemed to be bought and nothing to be sold." Both Honoré de Balzac and Sherlock Holmes were described in literature as possessing hoarding behaviors, including descriptions "of a collector of bric-a-brac" and "a horror of destroying documents" (Frost & Steketee, 2010, p. 61). Additionally, mythological stories about dragons indicate hoarding behaviors within this species. The book *Dragonology* describes both the *draco occidentalis magnus* and *draco orientalis* as having a love of treasures and using their lairs to store them as a survival technique to protect the soft unarmored areas on their bellies. "The dragons who evolved this hoarding behaviour were the ones who survived. Those who did not are no longer with us" (Steer, 2003, p. 16). A common thread between dragon and human behaviors of hoarding is this protection from vulnerability and the addictive covetous over-attachment to the hoard.

Before the rise of interest in hoarding behaviors, Sigmund Freud described behaviors in individuals that could be classified as part of this disorder. Orderliness, parsimoniousness, and obstinacy were a trio of traits that he believed resulted from anal fixation; Freud postulated that hoarding money, for instance, was symbolic of fecal retention (Frost & Steketee, 2010, p. 49). In classical psychoanalysis, Alfred Adler suggested that individuals who acquire possessions were compensating for a sense of inferiority created at birth, and that inanimate objects could provide comfort. This was demonstrated by Harry Haslow's experiments with infant monkeys, who preferred an inanimate, soft, cloth surrogate mother that provided no food over a wire-mesh one that provided food (Frost & Steketee, 2010, p. 50). The need for control equals the need for comfort when faced with a threat; fear is coupled with inadequacy, and inadequacy is coupled with improper attachments in early life. This is important given the long course of hoarding and its inception in early life for most people.

The term *compulsive hoarding* was first coined to distinguish normal saving and collecting from extreme, impetuous, and pathological acquisition. Currently, the DSM-5 (American Psychiatric Association, 2013) describes compulsive hoarding as having these characteristics:

1   Persistent difficulty discarding or parting with possessions, regardless of their actual value.
2   This difficulty is due to a perceived need to save the items and the distress associated with discarding them.
3   The difficulty discarding possessions results in the accumulation of possessions that congest and clutter active living areas and substantially compromise their intended use. If living areas are uncluttered, it is only because of the interventions of third parties (e.g., family members, cleaners, authorities).
4   The hoarding causes clinically significant distress or impairment in social, occupational, or other important areas of functioning (including maintaining a safe environment for self or others).
5   The hoarding is not attributable to a general medical condition (e.g., brain injury, cerebrovascular disease, or Prader-Willi Syndrome).
6   The hoarding is not better explained by the symptoms of another mental disorder (e.g., obsessions in OCD, decreased energy in Major Depressive Disorder, delusions in Schizophrenia or another Psychotic Disorder, cognitive deficits in major neurocognitive disorder, restricted interests in Autism Spectrum Disorder).

The disorder is considered to include excessive acquisition if symptoms are accompanied by excessive collecting, buying, or stealing of items that are not needed or for which there is no available space. There are three different levels of insight: (a) good or fair insight if they recognize that hoarding-related beliefs and behaviors (pertaining to difficulty discarding items, clutter, or excessive acquisition) are problematic; (b) poor insight if they are mostly convinced that hoarding-related beliefs and behaviors (pertaining to difficulty discarding items, clutter, or excessive acquisition) are not problematic despite evidence to the contrary; and (c) absent insight if they are completely convinced that hoarding-related beliefs and behaviors (pertaining to difficulty discarding items, clutter, or excessive acquisition) are not problematic despite evidence to the contrary.

Although there are some variations in descriptions of hoarding within other literature texts, most definitions resonate with the same themes. Nedelisky and Steele (2009) listed hoarding as a subtype of OCD, defined as follows: (a) the acquisition of and failure to discard a large number of possessions that appear to be useless or of limited value; (b) living spaces sufficiently cluttered so as to preclude activities for which those spaces were designed; and (c) significant distress or impairment in functioning caused by the hoarding (p. 365). However, people who hoard report feeling pleasure when they acquire special objects or find them amid their clutter, which is not usually associated with OCD characteristics (relief and not pleasure is associated with OCD). "He didn't organize or try to cull when he was there, he just enjoyed being amid his treasures. . . . When his gaze fixed on something he inspected it, and the effect was intoxicating" (Frost & Steketee, 2010, p. 208).

Also interesting is the etymology of the word *hoard*. According to the *Oxford English Dictionary*, the hoard *is* a treasure: "an accumulation or collection of anything valuable hidden away or laid by for preservation or future use, a stock, store, esp. of money." Simply stated, the mismanagement of one's relationship with objects through hoarding defines a level of crisis visible in an unmanageable house of clutter. The earliest use of the word *clutter* was in the year 1556, and Merriam-Webster (2013) defines the word as "to fill or cover with scattered or disordered things that impede movement or reduce effectiveness" or "a crowded or confused mass or collection." Either definition of the word *clutter* accurately describes the setting a hoarder inhabits with his or her objects. Limited living areas, small walkways, unusable bathrooms and kitchens, and objects stacked from floor to ceiling are common sights in spaces inhabited by hoarders. The need to acquire and keep things, even worthless things, can culminate in hazardous or unsanitary conditions, making a home unsuitable for humans. So, how did the definition of hoarding change to include defining and categorizing a person's treasure? I propose that it is not the value of the objects per se, but the process or purpose of the relationship with them.

The DSM-5 (American Psychiatric Association, 2013) diagnosis allows for a universally shared, symptom-based definition for the purpose of diagnosis and reference. Some researchers have pointed out that the term *hoarding* is of limited heuristic value. Symptoms or behaviors tend to define this disorder, which is likely a need for universally shared categories and a quick reference. Symptom listing often obscures explanation, and symptoms could overly dictate treatment. Mataix-Cols *et al.* (2010) clarify this statement by indicating that hoarding "can be a symptom of multiple organic and psychiatric disorders, and thus cannot be conceptualized as a single nosological entity or effectively guide therapeutic interventions" (p. 557). Furthermore, Maier (2004) concludes that there is not a consistent definition of the term *hoarding* and states that the term is used in different clinical and nonclinical contexts to explain various behavioral abnormities (p. 323). It is apparent that different theoretical modalities have their own definitions of hoarding and how to treat and prevent reoccurrences through medication, positive self-talk, and organizational skills, and that all yield high recidivism rates.

Simply stated, the acquisition and management of possessions that affect the owner is what defines the level of crisis hoarders find themselves in. Compulsive buying, compulsive acquiring of free things, or stealing is primarily how individuals collect their objects. According to numerous hoarding case studies, a majority of hoarders (20 out of 37 cases) describe tendencies to excessively acquire free things (e.g., free brochures, giveaways, and discarded items), and this was reported more frequently than compulsive buying (Frost, Tolin, Steketee, Fitch, & Selbo-Bruns, 2009, p. 633). Correlating research from Gilliam and Tolin (2010) also reports that individuals who hoard spend "inordinate amounts of time looking for and retrieving objects to take home, with behaviors that have included excessive spending or rummaging through trash bins" (p. 94). Individuals with hoarding tendencies have high levels of compulsive buying, such as purchasing extra items in anticipation of potential need or bargain buying for potential reselling purposes.

The most visible and striking aspect of a hoarder's problem is the extreme clutter, and the second most striking is ambivalence (difficulty with decisions/doubt)—having opposing beliefs or feelings about the objects he or she acquires. All hoarders seem to have ambivalence or doubt, that is, difficulty with decisions or inability to address opposing beliefs or feelings regarding their collected objects. People who hoard do not adequately explore and resolve this ambivalence, but instead, delay and avoid it with hoarding behaviors. Instead of not acquiring, they acquire, and instead of storing and using objects appropriately or releasing the objects, they leave the objects wherever they have an open area, creating disorder. The result of responding to doubt or ambivalence in this manner is excessive accumulation and clutter.

A hoarder does not see what has been gathered as scattered or disorganized. Individuals who hoard have exaggerated beliefs about their attachment to, accountability toward, and need to control possessions. They experience an increased level of anxiety when asked to discard items, take longer to decide if an item should be discarded, and may indignantly refuse to discard anything. "Discarding a book or newspaper might mean the loss of important information. . . . The possibility terrified her; it seemed it would be too much to bear, and perhaps it would" (Frost & Steketee, 2010, p. 156). Loss and grief replace the euphoria of collecting when their possessions are taken from them in a cleanup.

Research conducted by Tolin *et al.* (2010) indicates that the onset of hoarding behaviors emerges between 11 and 15 years of age, with most reporting onset before the age of 21; they further state that hoarding behaviors are mild in children but become more severe and prominent after 40 years of age (p. 835). The reasons, they postulate, are that (a) hoarding symptoms take several years to develop and severity increases over decades after onset, and (b) the presence of others in the home reduces the growth of clutter through their ability to limit acquisition, facilitate discarding of items, and force the removal of clutter. Insight into the processes and behaviors that hoarders engage in could be aided by exploring their developmental history and life events. According to Tolin *et al.* (2010), "Our clinical experiences suggest that as individuals who hoard leave their parents' homes or lose intimate partners through divorce or death, external constraints on hoarding behaviors are removed and the symptoms may become more severe" (p. 836).

Developing a treatment from symptoms of a disorder rather than from the processes that give rise to the symptoms could limit the treatment's effectiveness. More research is looking at contributory processes such as decision-making (ambivalence), creativity, perceptual detail, and distractibility, among others. For this reason, there has historically been resistance to treatment among individuals struggling with compulsive hoarding. There is some evidence to suggest that a solution-focused approach like cognitive behavioral therapy can yield favorable results with this disorder: "You and the therapist work together to learn how to sort and let go of possessions, think more clearly about your possessions, and control the urge to acquire" (Tolin, Frost, & Steketee, 2007, p. 7). However, can this simplified set of directions remedy a problem that originates on both a conscious and an unconscious level? Conventional therapy tactics include words like *self-discipline*, overnight homework that needs to be completed, aggressive cleanup, goals, deadlines, "keep" and "discard" piles, cleanup crews, keeping order, positive feedback to encourage discarding, and reviewing the plan logistics. A cleanup crew tears down the walls a hoarder has built as mental and physical protection from the real world of hurts. While the cleanup is taking place, the hoarder is defined as having legitimate issues but is strongly encouraged to give up control, which then re-traumatizes him or her and causes drama as the cleanup unfolds. This cannot be a healthy, therapeutic way of assisting a person with hoarding tendencies. Tolin *et al.* (2007) concluded that the number of people who are really "cured" within 8 months of therapy is low.

Medication has been introduced to combat hoarding tendencies as well. "Some new evidence suggests that some of the SSRIs (selective serotonin reuptake inhibitors) may be helpful for compulsive hoarding, but other evidence indicates that these medications are not as useful for treating hoarding as they are for OCD" (Tolin *et al.*, 2007, p. 8). So why does this treatment modality seem to be the most conventional way of treating compulsive disorders within our culture? Perhaps this is because there is no real understanding of the dynamics of hoarding and a lack of fluidity and creative imagination on behalf of the therapist. Exploring the imagination of the hoarder could yield surprising insights into the significance of acquiring things, then developing and maintaining a regimen of living with them. Therefore, it is important for new research to look at an even deeper process.

Both clinical psychology and depth psychotherapy agree on the fundamental principle that people who hoard have shown themselves to possess some type of psychological trauma; understanding the nature of the disorder is where they differ. This research is still a work in progress and is not accepted across the board, but it raises the question of whether trauma causes or simply exacerbates symptoms of hoarding. Both sciences can agree that progression and regression are important occurrences of psychic life and that progression consists of continually satisfying the demands of environmental conditions for an individual. "Progression could be defined as the daily advance of the process of psychological adaptation" (Jung, 1946/1960, p. 32). However, when progression becomes impossible, positive and negative can no longer unite in coordinated action, creating tension, which leads to conflict. Jung stated that this conflict led to attempts at mutual repression, which could lead to dissociation or disunion with oneself (Jung, 1946/1960, p. 33). Repression could also be a disallowing of the natural resilience that leads to growth in some processes that have been underutilized by the developing or evolving being. What is it in individuals that inhibits or does not allow for this organic process toward recovery in the service of greater adaptability?

> What the regression brings to the surface certainly seems at first sight to be slime from the depths; but if one does not stop short at a superficial evaluation and refrains from passing judgment on the basis of a preconceived dogma, it will be found that this "slime" contains not merely incompatible and rejected remnants of everyday life, or inconvenient and objectable animal tendencies, but also germs of a new and vital possibilities for the future.
>
> (Jung, 1946/1960, pp. 34–35)

Psychiatrists focus on treating the anxiety reported by a person with hoarding tendencies. Donald Kalsched (1996) cites Kohut while describing the anxiety phenomenon on a deeper level. Kalsched says the anxiety one feels in these states can be described as what Heinz Kohut calls disintegration anxiety—the deepest anxiety a person can experience. "It threatens the total annihilation of one's very humanity—the outright destruction of the human personality" (p. 34). Winnicott (1971) expanded on Kohut's anxiety theory by stating that frequent traumatic anxiety can foreclose a transitional space for a person with hoarding problems, replacing creative imagination with "fantasying"—a dissociated state that allows a kind of melancholic self-soothing, or "a defensive use of the imagination in the service of anxiety avoidance" (Kalsched, 1996, p. 35). Fantasying and idealizing objects to avoid the real pain of abandonment or isolation are at the center of a person's hoarding condition. Kalsched further emphasizes that people who repress affect or traumatogenic experiences do not feel an increase of power, independence, or enhanced function: on the contrary, they go numb, act out, somatize, or begin an addiction (p. 26). "We have observed a number of instances in which people hoard used tampons, nail clippings, even urine and feces—critical parts of themselves, from their [the hoarders'] point of view" (Frost & Steketee, 2010, p. 223).

This idea extends into the realm of psychology and the need to find treatment options for people who hoard, because mental health professionals cannot see an object for what it represents to the hoarder. The object might symbolize a frustrated attempt to renew the symbolic function. Hoarders unconsciously project their own feelings, attitudes, motives, and expectations onto the item, not allowing for objectivity, imagination, or metaphors to develop and pass into consciousness. Additionally, the feelings and attitudes they carry for the item are in fact the metaphors they are living by. The object becomes a fixed idea to the hoarder and a symptom to be treated by the psychologist. Contrary to that belief, James Hillman (1981) proposed that in fact the world's disorders are man-made enactments and projections of human subjectivity, and depth psychology is adamant that the pathology of the world out there is a result of the pathology of the world in here (p. 98). "Not only my pathology is projected onto the world; the world is inundating me with its unalleviated suffering" (Hillman, 1981, p. 90). Hillman further stated that the unconsciousness of the world is projected onto an individual and one cannot immunize or isolate an individual's soul against the illness in the soul of the world—it becomes a package deal. The hoarder's physical world is a mirror as metaphor for their internal world; this gets closer to the truth of things.

It is important to begin to recognize that knowledge can be seen as imposing some kind of order upon the reactions of a person's psychic system as it migrates into consciousness.

> Nobody drew the conclusion that if the subject of knowledge, the psyche, were in fact a veiled form of existence not immediately accessible to consciousness, then all our knowledge must be incomplete, and moreover to a degree that we cannot determine.
>
> (Jung, 1946/1960, p. 79)

Hoarding could be a misguided, but sincere attempt by the hoarder to become more conscious through matter. What is seen as resistance to existing treatment techniques could be an inability to fully comprehend what the hoarder is doing through these misguided processes. When a therapeutic relationship is encouraged with a patient, a healing process can begin, one that exposes the symbolic significance of objects, brings unconscious content into consciousness, and reduces anxiety by resolving the ambivalence that was avoided through hoarding. Through this set of processes, hoarders can become empowered and cease needing to use relationships with objects to manage what would otherwise make them feel powerless.

In our clinical work with patients, if we attempt to undermine a patient's life by imposing a cure, we enter into a treatment alliance/compliancy with them, allowing the client to escape us or give up the right to be alive and ill. Winnicott (1971) summed this up in his statement that the "absence of psycho-neurotic illness may be health, but it is not life" (p. 100). A depth psychological approach to hoarding can help a patient to remain living through an atmosphere of mutuality with a psychotherapist instead of attempting to rid them of their illness with the help of a cure. Ridding a person of hoarding tendencies is an admirable goal, but what, if anything, has been gained by the work? "And so we must free the vision of the psyche from the narrow biases of modern psychology, thereby enabling the psyche to perceive itself—its relations, its realities, its pathologies—altogether apart from psychology's modern perspective" (Hillman, 1975, p. 3).

The traditional psychological perspective keeps the hoarder from being fully seen because yielding a fixed idea about personality and insanity allows no space for the imaginal to be present and denies soul from appearing in events. Hillman refers to Henry Corbin when he says what imaginal means—the *mundus imaginalis*. "It is a distinct field of imaginal realities requiring methods and perceptual faculties different from the spiritual world beyond it or the empirical world of usual sense perception and naïve formulation" (Hillman, 1983a, p. 3). The imaginal allows for the locating of the archetype of the psyche, an imaginative phenomena, through their value and from their theophanic nature, virtuality, or potential.

Just like the hoarder, there is no space for the imaginal in the psychological perspective on treating hoarding behaviors. Words like *self* and *ego* are central to identifying an individual in psychological terms, but *soul* is not a word used in this discipline. Hillman cautions against dismissing or ignoring the imaginal, stating that not allowing freedom to imagine abuses the soul. By making space for fantasy or the imaginal, one can explore a path of discovery with no goals, but with openness to the luminous. Dennis Slattery (2002) cites Gaston Bachelard, from his book *Earth and Reveries of Will*, that things dream, nature dreams, and the substance of the world's body has its own imaginal qualities such that we who explore them are engaged more in a process of discovering than we are in invention. He continues by saying that Bachelard coined the term *dynamic imagination* for the process of exploring the inner recesses of the qualities that give things their life and dynamism in the world, which is achieved through an open heart and a willingness to be seduced. This is the process that allows hoarders to be seduced by the potential of an object, and this must be the task of the therapist as well. With an openness to the imaginal and space to dream, both hoarder and therapist can discover the individual processes they journey through with their objects. By experiencing an image from the point of view of the dynamic (material imagination), we allow the object to have a voice, to speak its own story.

2

IDENTIFICATIONS AND PROJECTIONS PLACED ON OBJECTS

There are commonalities in behavior between hoarders and mythological dragons. Both dragons and individuals who hoard conceal their possessions in cave-like settings; trust is needed before entering the lair of a dragon or the home of a hoarder, and one must have a highly respectful attitude when in the presence of their hoard (objects), or their sense of safety is jeopardized, creating negative behaviors in both species (Steer, 2003, pp. 17–18).

Whether we know it or not, something larger than ourselves is directing the steps that we take in our own personal journey. The creation of a myth helps a person know what to live by. "It generates a work, a lifestyle, and a meaning through which I am related to the living process of my own psyche and it is related it to me" (Bond, 1993, p. 24). Imagination and lifestyle is where a person's myth comes alive: a person's fantasy becomes a way of life. Inside ourselves is where myth lives, and there is a distinct connection between the myths that inform our lives and our way of life. Joseph Campbell (1988) eloquently defined myth in *The Power of Myth* as "stories of our search through the ages for truth, for meaning, for significance" and stressed the importance of telling and understanding our own stories and the "need for life to signify, to touch the eternal, to understand the mysterious" in order to comprehend who we are (p. 4). Through the disorientation hoarders find themselves in, psyche itself is seeking a new relationship between object, setting, and the myth the person is living by. Myth equals meaning, and meaning is mythological. "Every myth, however peculiar or exotic, contains the potential for revealing indirectly some unforeseen or neglected aspect of the human psyche" (Walker, 2002, p. 5).

Myth allows individual moments of a hoarder's life to create a story, a plot. Instead of treating the condition of hoarding as symptomatic of anxiety and OCD tendencies, exploring the personal myth that people who hoard are living by and seeing their condition more symbolically could lead to adaptations in their healing process. The personal myth hoarders live by is one of value and worth seen through the potential of their objects. The more they possess, the more of their life can be recorded, helping them achieve a sense of self. "To stop would make all those years [of collecting magazines] a waste of my life. It would make my existence invalid. I'm collecting life without living it" (Frost & Steketee, 2010, p. 117). When people focus on doing things to achieve purposes of outer value, they miss the rapture that is associated with being alive, which can be achieved if they concentrate on their inner value. According to Campbell (1988), being alive is what it's all about.

Bond (1993) has insightfully noted that "in order to experience myth, we first must come to terms with symbols" (p. 78). A common trait among hoarders is their dependency on the visual connection with objects they acquire and have literalized all dimensions of their life. Carl Jung considers all things—natural objects, man-made things, and abstract art—to have symbolism, and states that everything has symbolic significance tracing back into history. "Man, with his symbol-making propensity, unconsciously transforms objects or forms into symbols (thereby endowing them with great psychological importance) and expresses them both in his religion and his visual art" (Jung, 1964, p. 257). Due to this symbolism inherent in objects, people who hoard have a tendency to confuse their possessions with their emotions. "An object bears witness to itself in the image it offers, and its depth lies in the complexities of this image" (Hillman, 1981 p. 103). Bond (1993) elaborated on this idea in his book *Living Myth*; he stated that exploring the symbol leads one deeper into the psyche, "like a twig in the ground, into the roots of the psyche under the firm earth of reason" (p. 78). Symbols are irrational, concrete, specific, and multivalent. Symbolic consciousness commingles and sees comparisons; it unites in a profound way and does not tolerate objective consciousness. Mystery and potential are brought forth through symbol, "the patterns of objective, impersonal psyche from which what we experience as conscious contents are derived" (p. 89). The symbol, when met with imagination, becomes a window into the soul. The hoarder might have as intention to reclaim some of this, but struggles to see through this window covered by their clutter.

Paxton (2011) provided a metaphoric description of a hoarder's collection: "A pile in a hoarder house isn't a pile of stuff; it can be many things: a pile of sadness, a pile of quitting, or sometimes a pile of hope" (p. 41). According to Nedelisky and Steele (2009), an emotional connection is one of the four central constructs (identity, safety and security; a way to be connected to the world; value of the object and ownership or private, intimate; and idiosyncratic talisman of memory and desire) that mediate hoarders' relationships to inanimate objects; however, patterns of attachment to people or to these objects have not been formally studied (p. 366). Often people who hoard find their pleasure in their ability to acquire possessions—acquiring has become their only way to feel happy. Deriving pleasure from looking at, using, or showing off the items appears to be another common theme for people who struggle with excessive acquisitions, as is their ability to see and appreciate the creative potential of objects and features that others overlook.

This is called *projection*—confusion of object and subject, outer and inner. "Something on the inside, a piece of myself, is perceived on the outside—projected onto an object" (Bond, 1993, p. 7). The inanimate objects a person hoards become mirrors of sorts, reflecting an image in the person back to the person. The ambiguity the person projects onto the objects allows him or her to become significant and important.

Bond recalls that the term *participation mystique*, coined by French sociologist Lucien Levy-Bruhl, describes this phenomenon of subject with object.

> Considered psychologically, the experience of participation mystique is bound up with a subjective perception of intensity, usually an emotional and physical intensity. Perhaps the greater the intensity, the more likely it is that objects will be experienced as having a life of their own.
>
> (Bond, 1993, p. 9)

Psychological reactions to trauma experienced by an individual play a key role in this phenomenon.

> For hoarding, every object is rich in detail. We disregard the color and hue of a magazine cover as we search for the article inside. But if we paid attention, we might notice the soothing effect of the colors, and the meaning of the object would expand in the process.
>
> (Frost & Steketee, 2010, p. 15)

According to these authors, the underlying premise of hoarding is not about how much stuff a person has, but rather about how they process things. In a life overtaken by hoarding, individuals tend to come up with idea after idea about the objects they acquire, stating that they are saving the items for all types of creative reasons. Objects fire up the imagination of a hoarder. "Whenever she saw something that she thought might make a great gift, she purchased it, even though she had no particular recipient in mind" (Frost & Steketee, 2010, p. 21). This gives the hoarder another excuse to purchase more in the name of anonymity and creates motivation for saving items to create a private identity and not a public one.

Slattery (2002) stated that the phenomenologist and philosopher of science Bachelard's major goal was to collapse the distinction between inner subjectivity and outer material reality, which is very poignantly needed to help hoarders make sense of the chaos created by their objects. According to Slattery, Bachelard concluded that a substance, a texture, an image, or an element (either experienced directly or read in a literary work like a poem) throws individuals into a dream state. This dream state is where analogy, correspondence, and metaphor take over and seize individuals, allowing entrance into the poetics of the image, where memories from the past and from a more ancient primordial history rise up to alter their grasp of the most simple things (Slattery, 2002, p. 4).

A feeling of safety and security is another principle behind hoarding. "We have met people who describe their possessions as a 'nest' or 'cocoon' that makes them feel protected from what they perceive to be a dangerous world" (Tolin *et al.*, 2007, p. 37). They unconsciously seal off the inside of their homes to obtain a cocoon-like feeling of comfort and safety. The connection between objects and meaning becomes impermeable due to a strong need to maintain control over their possessions, which they perceive as the source of their safety and security. "Irene's 'treasures' helped her feel safe; when threatened, she wanted to surround herself with them" (Frost & Steketee, 2010, p. 85). Losing their objects fills hoarders with fear.

To people who hoard, objects are a way of being connected to the world. Their objects connect a hoarder to something bigger than themselves, an expanded identity, possibly a more meaningful life. In a hoarding situation, they tend to see their objects as giving them a sense of self, defining their worth by what they own and what they can do in relation to the objects, directing their value outward. The objects hold so much possibility for the hoarder. Tolin *et al.* (2007) suggest that most people define themselves by what they do, but people with hoarding problems often define themselves by what they have (p. 37). It is usually not the object itself, but rather the connection it symbolizes, that matters most to a hoarder. To a person who hoards, an object represents an opportunity and chance to experience something meaningful. "For some people, these items serve as a tangible record of their lives; throwing them away feels like losing that part of their lives" (Tolin *et al.*, 2007, p. 36). They appear to have no gap between having and being—they become one thing.

> When you find an active projection, find yourself relating to an object in an emotional way, you can dig up the subjective link, the connection to a buried yearning, hurt, or attachment, through the process that Jung called fantasy thinking, or non-directed thinking.
>
> (Bond, 1993, p. 11)

Associated patterns link experiences instead of logical concepts, therefore, it matters what one chooses to hoard due to the patterns in their matter.

Many hoarders see special value in society's unwanted trash and "rescue" items they claim have potential. This could be a mirroring of their own discarded selves, seeing their own potential that maybe no one else sees or understands; they create their life stories through their objects. Each possession acquired by a compulsive hoarder carries a story. Ownership of the objects and stories they represent seems to be a common theme in the research on hoarders and their objects (Frost & Steketee, 2010, p. 46). For this reason, individuals who hoard become emotionally and sometimes physically upset whenever someone touches their objects or attempts to remove them from their homes. In the book *Stuff*, Frost and Steketee (2010) described a hoarder trying to save his possessions from being cleared out: "Finally he darted into the apartment, jumped onto a cleared coffee table, and started yelling at one of the cleaning crew to put down a broken lamp" (p. 180). How does one create such strong feelings towards an object? Perhaps it is something primal where all objects possess a numinous quality, and therefore it is taboo to touch and pollute them.

> Of course, things are dead, said the old psychology, because they do not "experience" (feelings, memories, intentions). They may be animated by our projections, but to imagine their projecting upon us and each other their ideas and demands, to regard them as storing memories or presenting their feeling characters in their sensate qualities—this is magical thinking.
>
> (Hillman, 1981, p. 103)

Jung (1946/1960) stated that if thinking fails as the adapted function, because it is dealing with a situation to which one can adapt only by feeling, then the unconscious material activated by regression will contain the missing feeling function, although still in embryonic form, archaic and undeveloped (p. 36). Simply stated, hoarders need to adapt to the inner world of the psyche, which is primarily done through regression and activating an unconscious factor. The problem lies in that the hoarder becomes engulfed and reaps the harmful effects of such complexes due to not understanding, assimilating, or integrating the complexes into the conscious mind. People who hoard often try to mitigate or avoid suffering through accumulating objects, keeping it external in the form of things. However, in exchange for avoiding the actual conflict, a hoarder then suffers from a pseudo-problem and its symptoms. "Often he shows an almost inconceivable attachment to his complexes, even when he seems to suffer unbearably from them and to do everything in his power to get rid of them" (Jacobi, 1959, p. 18). In a hoarding situation, individuals who struggle with acquisition have verbalized that they feel the objects, not they, are in control. The objects both possess and control them. Lepselter (2011) made a valid assessment of a hoarder's home over time, stating that "hoarders' goods clearly have gotten the upper hand over order, and they often are no longer recognizable as goods at all" (p. 925). To outsiders who view a hoarder's home, filth and disorganization are noticeable, but the owner of the residence sees numerous treasures properly stored for future use. A hoarder's belief system dictates what they see; this is what myths do as well.

Objects that a hoarder acquires become more than themselves, although they do not obtain value in their exchange. "They [objects] are private, intimate, and idiosyncratic talismans of memory and desire. No one else wants them; they cannot be circulated or exchanged; they are trash" (Lepselter, 2011, p. 943). Elaborate processing of objects allows hoarders to think of numerous (creative) uses for a single object. A person with hoarding tendencies can see potential in an object like a broken lamp, thinking of numerous ways they can salvage the item and make it useful; however, to others not struggling with the disorder, it is just a broken lamp that does not work.

If an object carries personal symbolism for a hoarder, how can a prescribed treatment regimen create healing? Even the same symbol requires different interpretations with each individual person who hoards. The individual symbolic significance of each object to the hoarder requires individualized interpretation. The individual's neurosis transforms the object into a symbol. A symbol, for the hoarder, possesses meaning (rational or irrational) and can be interpreted from a subjective or objective viewpoint. From the Jungian perspective, a symbol is the psyche's best attempt to represent a psychic factor that is only partially knowable. So foreclosing the symbolic function denies the hoarder access to the dynamism of the unconscious, thereby stimulating the hoarder's thinking about material possessions as living symbols, which informs the hoard with new dimensions of meaning.

According to Dr. Suzanne Chabaud, a clinical psychologist who specializes in treatment of OCD and hoarding disorder and an expert consultant on the show *Hoarders*, the symbolism placed on an object by a hoarder can speak a language that is sometimes hard to describe in words. This allows the object to carry a meaning beyond the physical attributes. This process is universal. According to Jung, there are certain types of symbols that are universal, and resonate with the human unconscious. The goal is to discern where the universality of a symbol ends and the individual matching of a symbol to an object begins. Objects offer a range of potential symbols, perhaps limited to what a certain object affords by the very nature of the object (S. Chabaud, personal communication, 2013). The autonomy of the unconscious process, per Jung, has an abundance of images, and a person's psychic background possesses an untiring symbol-creating power (Jung, 1964, p. 374). Bond (1993) states that when people lose themselves in the complete identification of an object, they live the tyranny of objectivity with too much objective consciousness; this brings forth the loss of soul that makes people neurotic, for the loss of imagination is also the loss of soul (p. 16). Therefore, understanding the symbolic nature of hoarders' objects can lead to healing when they are given space, support, and guidance to interpret their own projected shadow material in their objects.

Mary Douglas, author of *Purity and Danger* (1966), made a sweeping claim that everyone universally finds dirt offensive, but it is what counts as dirt that allows for discussion and classification among people (p. xvii). "There is no such thing as absolute dirt: it exists in the eye of the beholder. If we shun dirt, it is not because of craven fear, still less dread of holy terror. Dirt offends against order" (p. 2). If what is classified as dirt is in the eye of the beholder, then shame can be projected onto hoarders from individuals who feel they do not follow particular societal protocol regarding cleanliness. Individuals' beliefs reinforce social pressure, according to Douglas, and individuals try to influence one another's behaviors (p. 3). Douglas pointed to an interesting idea: that dirt is matter that is out of place, never unique or an isolated event, but rather a system. The collective society defines the set of ordered relations and breaching of that order; therefore, dirt is the derivative of a systematic ordering and classification of order. She provided an example of this notion more clearly:

We can recognize in our own notions of dirt that we are using a kind of omnibus compendium, which includes all the rejected elements of ordered systems. It is a relative idea. Shoes are not dirty themselves, but it is dirty to place them in the dining room table; food is not dirty in itself, but it is dirty to leave cooking utensils in the bedroom, or food bespattered on clothing; similarly, bathroom equipment in the drawing room; clothes lying on chairs; outdoor things indoors; upstairs things downstairs; so on.

(Douglas, 1966, pp. 44–45)

In summary, society's classifications confuse or contradict our pollution reactions to condemn objects that are not categorized in the appropriate places. Furthermore, once objects are regarded as out of place, another transition happens, understanding their identity as unwanted pieces of something. "This is the stage at which they are dangerous; their half identity still clings to them and the clarity of the scene in which they obtrude is impaired by their presence" (Douglas, 1966, p. 197).

Once the object is recognized as dirt, its identity is lost in the long process of pulverizing, dissolving, and rotting. "The origin of the various bits and pieces is lost and they have entered into the mass of common rubbish" (Douglas, 1966, p. 197). Poking around in the refuse to recover anything is unpleasant. Once retrieved from the trash, the item regains an identity; therefore, if the identity remains absent, rubbish is not dangerous. Dirt is then utterly undifferentiated; total disintegration, and is therefore formless: per Douglas, an apt symbol of beginning and of growth as it is of decay (Douglas, 1966, p. 198).

Society's morals and values are forced upon hoarders, defining their dwellings as dirty, unclean, in disorder, and inhabitable. These projections laid upon hoarders allow for shame to creep in and inhabit their dwellings as well. Aristotle made an important distinction between the shame one feels about things that are offensive to "general opinion" and about things that are offensive to the "pure truth" (Lynd, 1961, p. 239).

The feeling state of shame has only recently been studied in psychoanalytic literature and was absent in Freud's writings. "One's knowledge of shame is often limited to the trace it leaves. Nevertheless, from Darwin forward, theorists have proposed the desire to hide or to disappear as one very important feature of the phenomenology of shame" (Lewis, 1992, p. 34). Figuratively, this is what individuals with hoarding tendencies achieve through their shame of acquiring too many objects that others think are useless: a cocoon to hide them. Hoarders become both objects and subjects of shame. Lewis continues to define this feeling state: "Shame disrupts ongoing activity as the self focuses completely on itself, and the result is confusion: inability to think clearly, inability to talk, and inability to act" (p. 34).

According to an article written by Gilbert and Andrews (1998) at the turn of the twenty-first century, Charles Cooley originated the ideas about the content of shame processing and coined the term *looking-glass self*. He stated that shame processing refers to the way individuals judge and feel about themselves according to how they think others judge and feel about them. Cooley categorized the looking-glass self into three cognitive aspects: the imagination of our appearance to the other person; the imagination of his judgment of that appearance; and some sort of self feeling, such as pride or mortification (as cited in Gilbert & Andrews, 1998, p. 17).

The term *mortification* is paramount to the discussion of shame and hoarders. The linguistic root of *mortification* is *mort*, defined as "to die." "Mortification may be internally or externally (publicly) induced; either way, it propels the person into hiding and concealment. At all costs, the source of the mortifying emotion must not be revealed" (Morrison, 1998, p. 53). Furthermore, from a depth perspective, Edward Edinger (1985) noted that *mortification* refers to the experience of death:

> [M]ortificatio is the most negative operation in alchemy. It has to do with darkness, defeat, torture, mutilation, death, and rotting. However, these dark images often lead over to positive ones: growth, resurrection, rebirth, but the hallmark of mortification is the color black.
>
> (p. 148)

With the visual imagery of darkness, defeat, and rotting that Edinger provides, one can see how death moves into a hoarder's setting through the emotion of shame. The hoarder's setting becomes a cocoon, a nest of sorts, facilitating the rotting decay of the old self, which mirrors the decay of material stuff.

Lepselter (2011) discusses the dirtiest element in a hoarder's environment as the objects themselves piled up out of order and writes, "Seen through the hoarder's eyes, the ordinary common sense divisions between purity and danger can themselves seem to slip; perhaps anything can shift from bounty to the grotesque" (p. 925). However, even in its ugliest and most grotesque form, the cocoon can be transformational for a hoarder, allowing metamorphosis into a new self through experiencing the objects from a symbolic position.

Theorist Erik Erickson set forth the classic theory of shame and observed a close connection between the origins of shame and the child's realization of its upright exposed position (Jacoby, 1991, p. 51). Shame is essentially a feeling of loathing against oneself and is an entirely personal and subjective reaction. However, certain categories of experiences inevitably generate it. Kalsched (1996) explains how a person's mind becomes "a tyrannical perfectionist, persecuting its weaker feeling-self, all the while hiding it as its shameful secret partner until finally, with all contact lost between the ego and this victim-self, a dreaded triggering word is mentioned ('Freemason')" (p. 95). Thus a person's ego is overcome by the abhorrent weakling inside, thrusting itself into becoming the only self, creating a world that is now identified by the person as tyrannical, persecutory, and perfectionistic (Kalsched, 1996, p. 95).

"Our internal struggles are not battles between instincts and reality, but conflicts that typically involve the understanding and negotiating of shame, its elicitors, and its frequency" (Lewis, 1992, p. 2). Shame requires self-awareness and an evaluation of one's actions, feelings, and behavior with a conclusion that one has done wrong. The intensity of the shame felt by an individual is in direct relation to the degree of differences in socialization of standards, rules, and goals. To feel shame, we compare our actions against another's standards or beliefs, thus bringing forth self-consciousness. Moreover, objective self-awareness of one's failures in relation to others' standards elicits feeling states of shame. If one chooses to concentrate on it, such states have a devastating effect on the self-system.

Feelings of shame can be hidden behind the semblances of anger, contempt, depression, denial, or superiority. It is what an individual is already aware of that causes the greatest distress when dealing with feelings of shame. "There is a sense, a conviction, a belief about the self that we find intolerable and that we try to manage by turning away in one way or another" (Morrison, 1998, p. 12). Mario Jacoby (1991) writes that a basic sense of being "unloved" in all spheres causes an underlying feeling of being utterly rejected, and this condition is accompanied by intense susceptibility to shame. "This prepares the ground for severe pathologies of every kind, from completely asocial to destructively addictive behaviors" (p. 51). Morrison (1998) affirmed that once people are convinced that they will be rejected and abandoned, they find little if any pleasure, esteem, or acceptance in their relationships and in turn feel shame about some aspect of themselves being unlovable and shame for being unloved and alone (p. 56).

One would imagine that conformity to standards and rules could be enforced through feelings of shame; however, sometimes extreme shame produces an aversive reaction and a change in behavior is not achieved. Blaming an internal instead of an external source produces higher levels of shame. Individuals have a difficult time dissipating the feeling of shame, and a global attack on the self begins. For this reason, shame is responsible for controlling our psychic direction. "Attention to the self is disruptive. The ability not to engage in objective self-awareness may be facilitated by an emotional concomitant that is intense and slightly aversive" (Lewis, 1992, p. 88).

When people enter the dwelling of a hoarder, disgust at their living conditions is present. Lewis (1992) confirms that one of the most painful experiences is another's display of disgust for one's actions, thoughts, or feelings (p. 110). The disgusted face of an onlooker peering in on the personal and private hoarded space produces shame for an individual struggling with this disorder. Empathic shame is felt between families of hoarders, allowing both to feel the same over the shame of another.

Individuals who acquire extensive numbers of objects verbalize distress at the sight of their clutter; feelings of embarrassment lead to avoidance of inviting friends and family to their home. A large-scale survey of participants who reported hoarding symptoms found high levels of social isolation and family conflict (Tolin, Frost, Steketee, & Fitch, 2008, p. 95). With their shame, hoarders tend to be isolated, cutting themselves off socially and emotionally even when they crave human interaction. "To engage in tactics of shame avoidance, one must have some sense that investing in avoidance strategies is worthwhile—that shame is so painful or deleterious to self that it must be avoided" (Gilbert & Andrews, 1998, p. 23).

Shame is a result of an early sense of unworthiness or rejection and lack of trust; trauma reactivates the unspeakable pain. "I think we can understand psychopathology by viewing love withdrawal as provoking shame and shame as leading to poor interpersonal relationships" (Lewis, 1992, p. 115). Objects hide the person sealed away from the *Other* and offer a false sense of protection, joy, and completeness or wholeness. When their hoarding pretense is exposed, they face the truth about their own endeavor, surfacing feelings of humiliation, inadequacy, and incompetence. In a sense, the lie is exposed. How can they admit that the pile of trash couldn't possibly take the place of the *other* after all? The shame that hoarders feel can be so intense that they withdraw from situations and people that evoke additional humiliation. They retreat into the darkness, the underworld, hiding from the way others see them. "The mask that we present to the world slips off and the face behind it becomes visible, with its expression of terror, greed, despair, dishonesty—whatever is usually kept in the cellar" (Tarrant, 1998, p. 44). The solitude and shame keep them stuck in the underworld for a while, sometimes for a lifetime; the only warmth they feel radiates from their objects.

Matt Paxton (2011) states that most hoarders are in pain from losing their connections with loved ones and family members. Ironically, the only way they see to ease their pain is to literally and figuratively bury themselves more deeply (p. 37). A pile of trash becomes a cocoon of safety, with interlocking objects throughout the living space of a hoarder's home creating a perceived veil of protection from all angles.

Many hoarders' self-images and self-worth have become dependent on the objects they believe represent them, creating a womb of safety that buffers them from outsiders. Hoarders' perceptions become their reality. "Someone filled with shame would like to force the world to look away in order to keep his shameful situation from being seen" (Jacoby, 1991, p. 53). Hoarders' settings and objects become their *prima materia*, the "gross aspect of life—unrefined, unredeemed by any admixture of spirit and yet a kind of foundation for all that follows, for all wisdom and art" (Tarrant, 1998, p. 68). The bottom substance of the *prima materia* in hoarders' settings and objects is experienced as disgusting and foreign by onlookers, with a heaviness and lack of form and organization that make entering the home and working in this environment difficult. The more resistance brought forth by hoarders and the more shame and pain they feel, the further into darkness they travel. Tarrant (1998) further states, "The ground of night doesn't have a direct voice and speaks in symptoms and pathology, including what we cannot bear about ourselves, asking us to acknowledge the despised and the dangerous as our own" (p. 68).

Individuals with hoarding tendencies mirror what is cluttering them on the inside, both psyche and self, in their hoards. The unattended shadow material that plagues people with hoarding tendencies can usually be found in their hoards; psychic clutter and residue can be found in physical form in piles of trash and the stink of rotting food or feces. Trinkets and mementoes of loved ones who have abandoned a hoarder provide solace and comfort for a broken heart and allow for the recreation of past good times to compensate for the present isolation. "The griefs of life beg attention; they are orphans, they want to be loved, they hold out their small hands, which grow larger and more substantial when we take them" (Tarrant, 1998, p. 77).

Attachment to the Other is what makes humans feel good—loving others and being loved by them. Ultimately, the creative interplay between the attachment object and the individual, "I want" meets "I get," both wanting and both giving, provides empathy in the exchange. Attachment provides a sense of companionship, affiliation, and love. However, according to John Bowlby (1980), disturbed patterns of attachment behavior can be present at any age due to development having followed a deviant pathway: "One of the commonest forms of disturbance is the over ready elicitation of attachment behaviour, resulting in anxious attachment" (p. 41). An affectional bond is essential to attachment behavior. When this is threatened in any situation, the bond educes actions intended to guard it. The greater the intensity of the loss for the individual, the more extreme and varied are the actions elicited to avert it. "One or more behavioral systems within a person may be deactivated, partially or completely. When that occurs one or more other activities may come to monopolize the person's time and attention, acting apparently as diversions" (Bowlby, 1980, p. 64). Could this be the reason why hoarders begin to acquire clutter and then have difficulty discarding it?

Monika Wikman (2004) describes the phenomenon of loss as occurring "when we lose connection with the spirit in the core of all beings" (p. xvii). She states that when this happens, an individual's consciousness becomes one-sided, dry, and cut off from the natural sources of renewal in the psyche. For people who hoard, their reactions are automatic and compulsive; they are possessed by an idea that they have difficulty expressing from a critical standpoint. They are "more or less caught in an archetypal automatism, which is accompanied by a feeling of fanaticism and absolute conviction" (Von Franz, 1988, p. 11). This is where Jung (1946/1960) states that psychic energy, a basic life-force that would manifest itself as needed, comes into play and is available to the ego complex and other unconscious complexes as voluntary motivation. Psyche and matter together create energy and are one. In *Psyche and Matter*, Von Franz (1988) states:

> It means that one should be able sometimes to drop all plans and duties imposed from the outside when the Self suddenly asks us to do something else and also that one can distinguish whether such demand comes from the Self or only from some other unconscious complexes.
>
> (p. 140)

Relinquishing plans and duties in service to the Self allows individuals to see if they are deficient or in synchronization with themselves and to use the luminosity that arises out of their complexes to connect to psyche.

According to Dr. Chabaud (personal communication, 2013), when the hoarder acquires and fails to discard a vast array of objects, the need to hoard is often expressed as a rigid drive to fulfill a number of intentions for the object. Despite this seemingly "well-intentioned" drive, the requirements to protect and properly handle the objects are often overlooked. Chabaud also stated that over time, and in more advanced stages of hoarding, long-saved objects often require disposal. This one-sided approach to relationships with objects, when transferred to inter-personal relationships, inhibits the hoarder's adaptation to the needs and desires of others. Chabaud believes that in a healthy relationship, interpersonal adaptations are well negotiated and the relationship evolves with mutual benefit. Most of the adult children of hoarders in Chabaud's research reported that their parents' need to control the flow of objects in the home overrode the interpersonal and physical needs and desires of the family. These research participants often didn't feel valued as children in their relationships with the hoarding parents and a sense of worthlessness persisted into their adult lives. Primarily, they did not feel noticed as unique individuals with relevant needs and wants (S. Chabaud, personal communication, 2013). Could this be because the parents' insight was so obscured by the amount of matter between them and their children? Bowlby (1980) postulates that our thoughts, feelings, and behaviors are linked to the circumstances we find ourselves in, but that this link may sometimes be missing or the wrong link may be made: "This cognitive disconnection of a response from the interpersonal situation that elicited it, I believe, to play an enormous role in psychopathology" (p. 67).

Chabaud, drawing on Jean Piaget's theory of cognitive development, expects that stopping longstanding hoarding behavior will place undue stress on existing internal structures. In over-assimilation, well-rehearsed operations involved in hoarding behavior are over-applied to life experiences. Information that could help the individual to evolve is simply disregarded or deemed irrelevant, until the limits of adaptability become visible in grave life impairments. To the outsider, the individual will be viewed as having compromised insight. The hoarder does not grasp opportunities to develop or exercise more adaptive operations and feels threatened by anything that challenges their point of view. When faced with a rapid clean-out, the hoarder will commonly return to hoarding behavior, sometimes with increased intensity (Frost & Steketee, 2010, pp. 96–97). When these schemas have reached a limit, disequilibrium occurs and they can no longer maintain the survivability of the organism. Without embracing opportunities to evolve, the hoarder will perish or experience a host of negative reactions including helplessness and depression. The goal of intervention is to assist the hoarder to develop more evolved schemas, operational or meaning making systems that can accommodate a broader range of information, challenges, emotions, and interactions, including an increased ability to tolerate discomfort and manage behavior toward meaningful and rewarding goals. In essence, equilibrium is restored by a change in internal schemas necessary for psychological evolution. The evolved individual can meaningfully assimilate new data with enhanced flexibility and adaptability (S. Chabaud, personal communication, 2013). Many individuals labeled hoarders have suffered failed relationships or the death of someone significant to them; many were abused as children or abused in a marriage (Paxton, 2011, p. 45). An acute state of mourning typically follows such losses. Identification with the lost person becomes the main process involved in mourning, and is compensatory for the loss sustained. Due to the painfulness of mourning, there is an insatiable and persistent yearning for the lost figure and perhaps a frustrated attempt to stop time. Anxiety is the response when the figure is believed to be temporarily absent, and pain and mourning engulf a person when the loss is permanent. Even after it is deemed useless, the urge to regain the lost person is still powerful and persistent.

> Main themes are that a mourner is repeatedly seized, whether he knows it or not, by an urge to call for, to search for, and to recover the lost person and that not infrequently he acts in accordance with that urge.
>
> (Bowlby, 1980, p. 28)

Hoarders engage in these very same acts, but from a fragmented and incomplete process, leading to identification with particular objects instead of healthy mourning. "Grief is a wound which leaves a scar, and that scar is forever etched in the fabric of the soul" (Romanyshyn, 1999, p. 7). The stripping away of hope accompanies despair. Despair begins the journey and drifting into darkness where the descent into the underworld slows, a paralysis and waiting of the soul to eventually begin the work of ascending back into the light. Addictions are birthed, and one loses connections and falls under the whims of the world. "Our attention is dispersed into objects and we struggle with the problem of our desire, which renews itself before it is completely satisfied" (Tarrant, 1998, p. 20). Soul plunges into emotions and the person searches for a reason for this pain, not through understanding, but seeking catharsis or an authentic story told through the images of their objects.

The loss of loved ones conceivably creates a need for hoarders to create defenses to hold on tighter to things. Melanie Klein believed that certain modes of defenses were to be understood as "directed against the 'pining' for the lost object" (Bowlby, 1980, p. 36). "During my visits to his home, when Ralph found something that had belonged to one of his parents amid his stuff, he made a stabbing motion to his chest to demonstrate how broken-hearted he was about their passing" (Frost & Steketee, 2010, p. 137). Robert Romanyshyn (1999), in *The Soul in Grief*, adds to Klein's belief with his firsthand account of the mourning process; he acknowledges that the slow process of grief and mourning possesses a rhythm, and when one refuses to adhere to the rhythm, one makes a monument of a past that no longer has a future. "In my grief I was forced to learn that the past matters only in light of a future and that without such an opening the past is a prison which locks you out of life" (Romanyshyn, 1999, p. 18).

Trusting after being badly hurt is a common problem among hoarders; their possessions are much safer and easier. "Sometimes, people hang on to something because they feel emotionally attached to it. Even though the item doesn't have much practical use, our sense of attachment can be a powerful motivator to hang on to it" (Tolin *et al.*, 2007, p. 158). Issues arise when a person forms an attachment to numerous items and can't seem to reduce the clutter, hanging on to the items at all costs even if they are dangerous or unhealthy to them. This could be because their objects take on a numinous quality or could be taboo objects that are a delight to cling to.

> He saved boxes of old photographs, knickknacks, and other family items that he felt someone would want someday. He also kept years' worth of church bulletins, linens, and discarded service accessories like candles and offering plates. He even had an original copy of *Playboy*, which may seem strange for a preacher, but maybe he thought it was a collector's item that would have future value.
>
> (Paxton, 2011, p. 31)

Tragedy among hoarders is common. Feelings of sadness, isolation, and being alone are defensive reactions to what has happened or what they believe has happened to them. Gilliam and Tolin (2010) report that individuals with hoarding behaviors have experienced a greater number of traumatic life events than non-hoarders (p. 96). Overwhelming despair seals a person off and precludes the help of others. Healing requires that the grieving person trust helping others or a connection with internal concepts of trust and the enduring results of a healthy attachment, as in object permanence, which a hoarder struggles with. "Reason and reassurance are ineffective because we are flooded with memories of other moments, now lost, that gave us our identity" (Carotenuto, 1989, p. 82). Therefore, hoarders turn to their objects for comfort and soothing reassurance and to return to an earlier time in their lives.

Loss and abandonment imprison hoarders in the solitude of their clutter. Withdrawal from others and a fierce possessiveness of objects arise out of a fear of living consciously as well as terror of annihilation, bringing forth greed and clinging dependency with clutter (Woodman & Dickson, 1996, p. 60). Donald Kalsched (1996) described this process using the image of a circuit breaker in his book *The Inner World of Trauma*: "If too much electricity comes in, i.e., more than the wires of the house can carry without burning up, then the circuit blows and the connection to the outside world is annihilated" (p. 23). Additionally, if no circuit breakers are operative, it will start a fire and burn the place down. Kalsched went on to explain how the psyche is much more complicated than a circuit breaker due to two sources of energy, specifically the outer and inner (unconscious) worlds of an individual. Both energies are shut off when the psychological circuit breaker blows. "The person must be defended against dangerous stimulation from the other world, but also from those needs and longings which arise from deep within" (Kalsched, 1996, p. 23). Impairment of the ability to make or maintain love relationships and to organize the rest of their lives allows hoarders to remain stuck in the never-ending piles of clutter—possibly the "neverendingness" is what the hoarder wishes for. Hillman (1975) expresses this idea in his book *Re-visioning Psychology*: "Destruction seeps out of us autonomously and we cannot redeem the broken trusts, hopes, loves" (p. 55).

James Hollis (1996) writes that when we lose a loved one, we need to grieve that loss and yet consciously value what we have internalized from that person (p. 45). For hoarders, their homes are cluttered with items that remind them of loved ones who have exited their lives. Fear of discarding good memories of these people, through their items, keeps hoarders buried in grief and cocooned in the illusion that they are honoring their loved ones. All the while they are really creating hazardous piles of stuff to compensate for the pain of losing their connections with loved ones and the world at large. "Death demolishes any hope we might have about overcoming loss or controlling its pain" (Romanyshyn, 1999, p. 53). Grief provides hoarders with a shield of protection, robbing them of security one builds from loss of love and the illusion of what they have, and the accumulation of their objects can isolate them from the world. Their shattered foundations are literally and imaginally rebuilt by reinforcing their dwellings with objects stacked high, holding up the foundation and ceiling. The house the hoarder calls home is the interior space one fills with mementoes and memories of the past in order to create an atmosphere of closeness.

According to Bowlby (1980), attachment behavior is conceived as any form of behavior that results in a person attaining or retaining proximity to some other differentiated and preferred individual (p. 39). Hoarders retain proximity to an absent loved one through an attachment to objects that represent the individual. Bowlby further states that as long as the attachment figure remains accessible and responsive, the behavior may consist of little more than checking by eye or ear on the whereabouts of the figure and exchanging occasional glances and greetings (p. 39). This is what hoarders do with their objects—observing, checking, touching, and conversing.

For a hoarder, the loss is not grieved but replaced by inanimate objects that provide comfort and value: inanimate objects that are *alive*, living things with feelings, objects in need of love or rescue. The objects that surround hoarders act as insulators, keeping them safe from the dangers of the world. Isolation from the world allows an individual that hoards to project all that is meaningful or useful onto their stuff instead of with intimate human relationships. As Romanyshyn (1999) states:

> There were sounds, smells, tastes, textures, but it was not me or my personal mind which experienced them. Instead, there was a kind of identification with them, so that in these moments the boundary between myself and the world disappeared.
>
> (p. 61)

People who hoard report increased emotions, sensations, and details related to objects they collect as if they are creating relationships with inanimate objects. The profound effects of loss can change an individual into what seems like another person—someone unlike the one others had known previously, someone who has lost their grip on the world. "Safe behind the piles, where nobody will reach out and try to engage them in a healthy relationship, hoarders don't run the risk of being hurt again" (Paxton, 2011, p. 45). Matt Paxton (2011), owner of Clutter Cleaner and a popular expert on hoarding, concludes that, "the only way they see to ease their pain is to literally and figuratively bury themselves more deeply" (p. 37).

3

MEDIA INFLUENCE AND CONSUMERISM VERSUS HUMAN SURVIVAL

Who defines what is considered trash? Depending on cultural and personal value systems, what is considered pure or impure, edible or spoiled, trash or antique is debated and revealed in the media for all to judge. Ideas of what should be discarded change over time and vary from place to place, according to individual as well as collective preferences. According to Susan Strasser (1999), author of *Waste and Want*, categories of objects used and thrown out are fluid and socially defined; objects move in and out of these classifications depending on a person's sentimental attachment or ideology of frugality (p. 8). In her book, she provides a thorough look into American's evolution of consumerism and trash-making propensity by describing how manufacturers took advantage of technological advancements that created technological obsolescence for mostly wealthy consumers; in the process they created a demand to replace goods before the old ones were used up. "The accelerated obsolescence exercised by the wealthy increased the standard of living of the poor" (Strasser, 1999, p. 196). This could have been considered a good thing, depending on one's point of view.

In 1929, Christine Frederick, author of *Selling Mrs. Consumer*, explained that there was nothing civilized or cultured about holding onto old objects or things because it discouraged designers from creating new items, inventors from inventing new objects, and businessmen from offering new things (pp. 249–250). Richardson Wright, in his 1930 article written for *House & Garden Magazine*, expressed the same sentiment: that in order for a man to labor and earn a wage, the machine must keep working and functioning, and that good citizens do not repair the old, they buy new. With that type of thinking during that era, most families moved towards a modern relationship to the material world. This style of thought has progressed into the present day: making fewer things, buying more, saving and fixing less, and throwing out more.

> The taste for novelty, the conviction that new things represented progress, and the belief that products were desirable because they represented modernity contributed to the celebration of the modern way. It all added up to well-being, a luxurious life without annoyance or worry.
>
> (Strasser, 1999, pp. 199–200)

Buying and owning the newest stuff proved to be a potent magnet to the American people by transforming their relationship to waste and consumerism—another iteration of keeping up with the Joneses.

In *Waste and Want*, Strasser (1999) provides further details on how consumerism was fostered during the Great Depression. Economists blamed under-consumption as the reason for the Great Depression and suggested that if people just spent their money, the hard times would improve. New colors, designs, and packaging were created to entice consumers to spend with attempts to conquer under-consumption; incentives were even provided to consumers as a reward.

> People in the advertising business were explicit about their intent to get consumers 'to abandon the old and buy the new to be up to date,' in the words of a top advertising agent Earnest Elmo Calkins, writing in 1932.
>
> (Strasser, 1999, p. 205)

Postwar consumerism shifted to attract the notion of "disposability" by using terms like *freedom* to convey the idea of convenience; this soon became advertising's selling point. The consequence of this type of thinking was a collective ignorance of what happened to household trash. Sanitary landfills were introduced in the 1930s to deal with the dilemma of disposable items. Present day landfills are now analyzed by archaeologists to examine disposal habits, using artifacts that did not decompose as fast as originally thought. Strasser provided an example of this concept: "The city engineer of Bismarck, North Dakota, discovered in 1965 that a paper [receipt] had scarcely decomposed in the landfill he excavated in the course of building a new highway to the airport," (p. 272). He also reported that he uncovered a receipt for groceries, which had a legible date of 1920.

Vance Packard (1960) in *The Waste Makers* coined the phrase "throw away spirit" and warned consumers of this type of behavior; he went on to describe them as "credit-dependent hedonists" (p. 41). Giroux (2014) states that people surrender their citizenship when public values are disdained and public good and civic imagination disappear; "In turn, they are rendered disposable becoming the waste products of a society increasingly wedded to throwing away not just consumer products, but human beings as well" (p. 79). For this reason, public values are weakened, turning the principles of democracy on themselves and cracking the infrastructure of social solidarity.

Around 1969–1974, Americans hit another recession and garage sales became a fad; however, by the 1990s garage sales were considered an institution, generating over a billion dollars a year in over six million households. "Rather than a sign of a troubled economy, garage sales were a function of affluence, a response to the proliferation of stuff that Packard had described" (Strasser, 1999, p. 281). Strasser also stated that because of bigger houses, the invention of mini storage facilities, and discarding items through garage sales, Americans freed up more space to continue their often exorbitant consumption. In the language of community, social justice, and challenge to the capitalist system during the 1970s movement of consumption, many used radical rhetoric and the ideas of counterculture to describe garage sales. However, today, garage sales and flea markets enable both shedding hoarded objects to make room for more desirable current year items as well as the desire on the part of consumers to gain more for less.

Individuals keep consuming, whether they need to or not. A consuming culture, bereft of other forms of nourishment, creates a neurotically obsessed hoarding culture. There seems to be the beginnings of a cultural move to have individuals forget liberal arts learning, the humanities, critical thinking, discernment, and the value of a generally informed citizenry, which leads individuals into a small corral of purchasing, consuming, and gorging on distractions. Henry Giroux (2014), author of *The Violence of Organized Forgetting*, shares this sentiment: "As the pleasure principle becomes less constrained by a moral compass based on a respect for others, it is increasingly shaped by the need for intense excitement and a never-ending flood of heightened sensation" (p. 51). Advertisement and marketing firms develop branding techniques to attract consumers and to influence consumer behaviors with the latest gadgets that provide a relief from present day stressors. Giroux believes that nonstop marketing reduces the sense of agency to the imperatives of ownership, shopping, credit, and debt in a culture that once sought to open the imagination but now dispels it (p. 10).

What about individuals who rebuke the notion of consumerism but are still dazzled by the gleam of consumption? For scroungers and gleaners, community and street life unfold through a series of practical opportunities. They scour every corner, walking through the streets more than once, determined through dedication and existential seduction to retrieve all items dumped that can be repurposed, recycled and have value. Items found in trash cans and on street corners are remnants of an abundance of consumption and consumerism, tossed out due to age, lack of function, tragedies, memories, and endings or changes in personal status.

> In its daily rhythms, the empire of scrounge demonstrates once again that "the cultural" is not generated only by the operations of the mass media or the machinations of moral entrepreneurs; it pervades even the most commonplace worlds, animating the bottom of the social order as surely as the top.
>
> (Ferrell, 2006, p. 203)

Gleaning, the act of collecting leftover crops from a farmer's field after harvest, was considered a noble profession in the past:

> Since 1554, when King Henry IV affirmed the right of gleaning, it has been a practice protected by the French constitution, and today the men and women who sift through the dumpsters and markets of Paris are the descendants of gleaners who were painted by Millet and Van Gogh.
>
> (Ebert, 2001, p. 1)

In 2000, Agnes Varda produced a documentary film called *Gleaners and I*, which depicts her travels throughout the French countryside showing the gleaning of everything from potatoes to grapes, apples to oysters. It included urban gleaners—individuals repurposing and recycling items and solely feeding themselves from gleaning. She provided an intimate look into what the French saw as a useful profession.

> In general, one of the film's most appealing features is its democratic treatment of its interview subjects, who range from gypsies and unemployed young people to magistrate and a psychotherapist; they're all respected equally, and Varda lets them speak for themselves without passing judgment.
>
> (Wilson, 2002, p. 2)

Varda described a true gleaner as a little noble, idealistic, stubborn, and deeply thrifty.

Linda M. Hasselstron, in "Gleaning with Mac" from the book *Going Green* (Pritchett, 2009), states that gleaning for her is a discipline, a doctrine that she pays close attention to, and a philosophy as well as a method. She states that gleaning is more than scavenging or saving money to her: it is an ethical duty (Pritchett, 2009, p. 9). Individuals glean for numerous reasons—survival, choice, being forced into it, learning to love it—but all with the purpose of one item flowing into another and for a society where things find numerous uses. It raises the question, from the standpoint of culture and priorities, of the levels of environmental consciousness among those who glean and those who do not.

Scroungers are individuals who obtain items through salvaging or foraging. There are many forms of scrounging. Garbage picking is the practice of sifting through commercial or residential waste to locate useful items. Additionally, dumpster diving is the practice of scrounging from Dumpsters for clothing, furniture, food, and anything that is in good working condition or can be repurposed. There is even a profession called garbologists: people who study the sociology and archaeology of trash in modern life. Some dumpster divers self-identify as freegans, living exclusively from scrounged goods in an attempt to reduce their ecological footprint. Other words like *skipping, binner, containering, D-mart, dumpstering, tatting,* or *skip dipping* have been used to refer to salvaging what others deem as trash. It is interesting to note how the vocabulary tries to identify them.

A person can live solely off of what they scrounge daily from trash bins and Dumpsters: food, clothes, furniture, and items to recycle for additional cash. Jeff Ferrell (2006), in his book *Empire of Scrounge*, presents a provocative, insightful question: "For every object that I and every other scrounger can manage to scrounge, every day in Fort Worth or any other city, how many more make their way each day to the landfill, untouched and unclaimed?" (p. 33). In a nation consumed with materialism and consumption—out with the old technology and in with the new, even if it is only one year old—trash accumulates at a startling rate. We are saturated with material culture. The bountiful assortment of items left curbside can meet various needs and desires of scroungers and their pets, family members, and friends. With so much trash being discarded, it is disappointing that society condemns and casts shame upon those taking advantage of the free surplus sitting curbside waiting for its final resting place in a landfill.

Agnes Varda, in "Trash and Treasure" (Wilson, 2002), implies that gleaning is a form of resistance in a more broad sense because it is refusing to be boxed in by conventional expectations, allowing for individual creativity and initiative through re-learning age-old skills. Ferrell (2006) echoes the same value system. He explains the shared culture of scrounging as having a code of honor, with common values of reinvention and mutual aid. Both practices seem to yield positive outcomes for the environment and individuals by decreasing the amount of barely- used consumer goods clogging landfills and placing them into the hands of scroungers and gleaners, sustaining them for a lifetime.

Sadly, though, Ferrell (2006) details that in many cities scrounging is considered illegal and punishable by fines and jail time. Depending on the city, curbside trash is considered to already belong to the city trash hauling services or to be the property of the Dumpster owner, and scroungers are therefore prohibited from combing through it. "Many city governments now prohibit homeless folks and other city residents from scrounging in Dumpsters and downtown trash cans, arguing that such activity constitute 'offensive conduct in a public place'" (Ferrell, 2006, p. 11). It is absurd that an attempt to save the environment by repurposing items left curbside would be considered offensive. Additionally, the traditional practice of gleaning has largely been deemed illegal due to liability issues for farmers related to the safety of the food and the fields. Legal red tape and cultural and social stigmatizations seem to prevent urban scroungers from surviving and thriving and also prevent our environment from doing the same. In a collective society, people whose main objective is to live off what others discard should be viewed as helping to sustain our environment, not requiring punishment.

Scroungers and gleaners attempt to use and reuse and find purposeful meaning in old items, or use them to create new ones. Libby James, in *Going Green*, phrases this sentiment eloquently: "I think it satisfies something deep inside of me to see how long an item can remain useful and to figure out new ways to use things that would otherwise meet their end in the trash heap" (Pritchett, 2009, p. 71).

A person's trash can be seen differently depending on class, ethnicity, and family values. Throughout the world, customs and rituals have been established that include ways of handling excess, thus keeping it out of the trash. Nomadic people must travel light so they save less; Scots are known for value saving and reusing items, older people in the twentieth century conserve more due to living through the

Great Depression, and young people adopted ideals of convenience and disposability (Strasser, 1999, p. 9). Strasser defines the cultural and personal debate on trash by indicating that Americans consider rotting and rancid organic material impure; however, the line between rancid and fresh, edible and spoiled, pure and impure is where the differences lie (p. 4). The dynamic nature of the category "trash" suggests there is a personal component to defining one's belongings; the sorting process that creates this trash can vary depending on person, place, and time. However, Strasser suggests that we must also consider "the categories of objects we use and throw out are fluid and socially defined, and objects move in and out of these classifications," (p. 8).

The media in American society is a good place to see this dynamic dramatized. The general population should organize social movements, not money and corporations. However, media is one example were the nature of politics and policies that allow critical modes of citizenship to be dictated by ratings that translates into money in the pockets of the corporation.

> Narcissism and sociopathic greed have morphed into more than psychological categories that point to an affliction of the marginal few. Such diseased behaviors are now symptomatic of a plutocratic society in which extremes of violence, militarization, cruelty, and inequality are hardly noticed and have become normalized.
>
> (Giroux, 2014, p. 193)

On television shows depicting hoarding, one person's trash is defined by the collective viewing society as a whole and the disorder of hoarding is sensationalized for viewing ratings. Giroux's description above captures what media corporations attempt to achieve through particular television programs designed to draw ratings and increase profits. Giroux details the media contribution to America's descent into madness by illuminating how mainstream media spins stories that are for the most part racist, violent, and irresponsible; they celebrate and demonize victims in the name of entertainment while hiding their pedagogical influence. "A predatory culture celebrates a narcissistic hyper-individualism that radiates a near sociopathic lack of interest in—or compassion and responsibility for—others" (Giroux, 2014, p. 9). Furthermore, he states that the media provide stories of cruelty and fear that undermine communal bonds and broadcast mutually related virtues of an unbridled market.

The A&E television show *Hoarders* (Chan, Severson, & Kelly, 2009) is exactly what Giroux describes. The show provides a 30-minute synopsis of each hoarder's life; then individuals attempt to clean up their home. This not only does a disservice to the hoarder suffering from a debilitating condition, but also provides an inaccurate picture of helping a hoarder clean out their home as a quick fix process. The show begins every episode with a caption: "Out of 3 million hoarders . . . these are two of their stories." *Hoarders* does not tell the whole story of a person struggling with hoarding tendencies, just a 30-minute glimpse highlighting the eye-catching details of the hoard with a small snapshot of the background life of the hoarder. The producers provide a synopsis of the loss and abandonment of their featured hoarder; however, they do not situate the loss through transitional objects (items used to provide *psychological* comfort, especially in unusual or unique situations).

A *Hoarders* episode begins with a quick introduction of the individual and his or her emotional traumatic background for the audience, and then moves on to show the clutter of the home. The show seems to contradict what is known about the shame and embarrassment associated with a hoarder's environment by placing hoarders in front of a camera lens, exposing them to additional shame from viewers.

The show waxes dramatic by showing problems associated with the hoarding situation, like the Crown Prosecution Service (CPS) removing children or family members abandoning the person if the home is not cleaned. An ultimatum is given to the hoarder to clean up or suffer the consequences of their behavior. Does this not reinforce their guilt, shame, and feelings of conditional love? Family members view the hoarder as someone who cannot let go of anything and believe that the individual is in denial about being a hoarder.

An example of this dynamic was aired on February 20, 2012. The story of Dee begins with a brief synopsis saying that since she moved into the house 10 years ago, no one has been allowed into the property, not even her daughter Talia. Her daughter recalls a time when she was 9 months pregnant and had to use the bathroom, but Dee told her no. Talia has been told that her mother cannot walk in the home, there is no running water, and Dee showers elsewhere. Interestingly, Talia lived close by and was aware of the fire hazard of the house being packed to the roof with a blocked entry, but has allowed the condition to persist.

Talia reports having known her mother was a hoarder since she was little; she recalls her mother living in the bathroom and leaving their dead cats in the freezer after they died because she couldn't let go of them. Talia states that she never reported her because she was afraid that Dee would pick hoarding over her. Dee says she doesn't have a problem and just needs to organize better. Talia has allowed her mother to use this excuse for years. However, in the episode she is no longer willing to tiptoe around the problem and says she will report Dee to authorities if she does not clean up.

The other story that aired in the same episode is about Jan, who lives in one room of her cat-infested home. The camera zooms in on the piles of cat feces that litter the furniture, floors, and kitchen appliances. The sensationalized drama begins as the background music changes in intensity and the camera zooms in on human feces in the bathroom toilet, which she has used for years with no running water, and human urine in gallon jugs. The story changes again with lower-intensity music, and Jan's past trauma and losses unfold, including how her hoarding affected her daughter and her daughter's need to distance herself from her. The story of Jan ends with more zooming in on the feces throughout the home and Jan crying about how ashamed she feels—all for the sensational, the dramatic, the abnormal.

Even though the show stars a licensed psychologist specializing in hoarding and OCD tendencies, and a professional organizer, no real therapy is provided to help the hoarders deal with the traumatic losses in their lives; rather, they suggest ongoing follow-up care at the end of the cleanup. However, there are occasions when some words of therapy are provided, both to educate viewers and as a brief effort to make sense of the hoarder's trauma as it correlates to their condition. The brief therapy, when conducted, is in the here and now, with an attempt to heal interpersonal relationships that have been broken due to the hoarding condition.

The clinical psychologist on the show states that the hoarder needs to quickly identify cognitive distortions about their need for stuff to avoid further consequences of their hoard. Family members and other invested parties employ threats to force hoarders to clean out their residences. They ask them to sort items faster, to see the bigger picture of where their stuff fits in their home and to decide whether objects have value immediately, sometimes not even allowing the hoarder to look at each item in the box. Loved ones are portrayed as victims of the hoard; however, most were not previously proactive with seeking help or understanding the disorder. Most times, family members and loved ones enabled the problem further by avoiding the person and his or her condition.

On the episode of *Hoarders* that aired September 13, 2010, the camera records attempts to sort through Ken's hoard by his estranged wife Noemi (who moved out in 2008), the clinical psychologist, and a professional organizer. The ultimatum given to Ken by the city included a large fine, the loss of his home, and jail time if he did not clean up his yard and house. Additionally, Noemi refused to move back into the home with their son until it was clean. The professional organizer says that Ken is dragging his feet, keeping things of no value, and Ken verbalizes that he feels they are stretching out the pain for him. The organizer says he is going to start telling Ken what are good decisions and bad decisions and what will keep him out of jail or send him to jail. He states that he is going to be more forceful with Ken until he can make decisions on his own. The psychologist states that they need to challenge Ken's thinking in the moment while going through his hoard.

Part of the treatment of hoarding, as a subset of OCD, involves dealing with an anxiety disorder that traps individuals in endless cycles of repetitive thoughts and behaviors. As clinically defined, hoarders struggle with OCD and are plagued with recurring and distressing thoughts and fears that they feel are uncontrollable. How, then, is it possible to challenge a hoarder's thinking in the moment when one's extreme anxiety keeps one from making sound decisions?

Due to the sensitive and embarrassing nature of the disorder, most hoarders don't verbalize how they feel to others, especially not publicly. This raises the question of where the television show found participants willing to be exposed to the guilt and shame associated with filming their emotional drama. People who hoard verbalize feeling safe in an unsafe world, feeling accepted when they feel they have been discarded by family and friends, and being able to hold onto their possessions when all else has been taken without their permission. Their home is a place for them to belong even if mounds of stuff encompass it.

Another reality show called *American Pickers* on the History Channel features two men, Mike Wolfe and Frank Fritz, who identify themselves as seekers for unusual and forgotten items that people have hidden within their private collections (Tremayne, Poertner, & Wolfe, 2010). The people are seen as individual collectors, not hoarders. The men are sent to different locations around the United States by their office staffer Danielle; they also conduct what they call freestyle stops at people's homes that appear to have a lot of stuff out front. They dig through decades and centuries of cultural history hoping to find a cornucopia of material culture; they pick through people's collections in their homes, warehouses, old general and antique stores, and outbuildings. These dwellings are defined as time capsules of valuable stuff and collectibles, but the collections are also items hoarded together. What is the difference between hoarders and collectors? Is it the neat organization of the collector's stuff, which is not mixed with the boxes and loose-leaf papers that accompany a hoarder's valuables?

Each *American Pickers* episode starts with the mantra that they are looking for rusty gold and amazing things buried in people's garages and barns. The show's premise is that what most people see as junk, they see as dollar signs, and they will buy anything they think they can make a profit from. This is definitely a different concept; they spin hoarding into collecting items with histories all their own and frame the people they meet as a unique breed of people. On the *American Pickers* episode from March 28, 2011, Mill is defined as a "pack rat" and the camera films his numerous boxes that are piled to the ceiling. Frank says that so far it is looking good and they love pack rats, and Mill states that he collects a lot of different stuff.

The camera selectively shows valuable items as key finds, but these key finds are usually nestled next to piles of things they try to avoid filming or discussing. Another interesting note relates to the location of the properties where Mike and Frank look for their pickings. A lot of the places are in rural areas on dirt roads, or large warehouses, not located in proximity to other residential houses. Does this make hoarding more acceptable and less scrutinized because it is not near other residential homes?

Unlike *Hoarders*, *American Pickers* casts people with excessive stuff in a positive light, as professional craftsmen or passionate collectors. The show does not show people trying to clean out their homes, or use disparaging language to describe them.

The July 15, 2013, episode "Bad Mother Shucker" shows a man's elaborate toy collection. Ellis's garage was filled up with stuff, so he built a general store on his property for all the toys he collected. He says he collects toys because of the joy of the hunt. Frank is astonished by his collection and says that no one builds a collection like this unless they are extremely attached to it. "I normally don't sell anything; I buy and keep. I guess I can be a hoarder," Ellis says in the episode. The next stop for Mike and Frank is a man who states that his kids and wife are fed up with his passion for collecting, as he makes a knife movement across his neck. When Mike and Frank go up in the rafters of the collector's garage, he says, "I don't even know what is up there." Both of these sentiments in the episode seem to ring true for hoarders as well: a passion for the find, the frustration of family, and not knowing what is in their collection.

The episode "The Royal Risk," which aired on May 27, 2013, features Pat, who begins his segment apologizing for the mess inside his home. Pat has a 1911 Flying Merkel sitting in his living room, which is packed to the ceiling with stuff. Frank makes a positive statement about the contents of the living room by focusing just on the motorcycle: "You are not just looking at a motorcycle, you are looking at a piece of art." Pat also has a 1910 Harley-Davidson motorcycle in another room with laundry, paperwork, and files on top of it; when Mike and Frank notice the motorcycle, he responds that if they gave him notice, he would have cleaned his place up. He refuses to sell either bike to Mike and Frank, saying there is "a lot of emotion attached." In another room labeled the scrap and dent area, he has a rusted partial metal frame from a 1910 Royal Pioneer motorcycle sitting on the floor in pieces. Mike offers him $40,000 and Pat returns a high bid of $60,000 in an attempt to hold on to the scrap piece of metal. Pat states, "It is hard to put a value on emotion." Rather than being negatively defined as a hoarder who is unable to get rid of anything, Pat is portrayed as a collector not wanting to sell the bikes because he understands their monetary value and knows he will never own another.

This is not about how the inside of an individual's home looks, but about how their items are viewed by others and the judgment and shame is kept on being projected onto those deemed hoarders by their family and onlookers. *Hoarders* allows others to define the value of the stuff people collect, while *American Pickers* allows the collectors to define the value of their stuff. Why is one considered more capable than the other? There are numerous similarities among the hoarders and collectors on these shows, but they are defined and classified differently. On the April 23, 2012, episode of *American Pickers*, Mike states that when he deals with scrappers and junkers, he reveres them as really smart people with great eyes. He says they know how to sort, they are able to see value in objects, and they know not to scrap them.

In the April 23, 2012, episode "Mike's Holy Grail," Betty has numerous warehouses on her property that house her father's collections. One building contains 500,000 hand grenade canisters, extensive WWII memorabilia of all kinds, old school desks and lockers, and items of all sorts piled high to the ceiling, both randomly and in cardboard boxes. How is this different from the *Hoarders* episode that aired on December 10, 2012, where Chris has eight storage units of stuff that he feels is of value? Chris states that he clings to what he finds comforting, mostly electrical and mechanical stuff that he finds on the street. Chris, like the individuals on *American Pickers*, describes enjoying the process of discovery. However, unlike Betty, Chris's sister considers his collection trash, asks what is the matter with him, and deems his situation ridiculous.

Television media has a powerful platform regarding how they want their audience to view their network shows. Tactics of sensationalism are employed by television producers to capture audiences and keep them hooked on a series. *Hoarders* focuses on the gross, chaotic, and disgusting aspects of a hoarder's home to draw and keep audiences, whereas *American Pickers* focuses on the treasure found within the hoard and the amount of money fetched for items picked.

Millions of people have been entertained by these two A&E television shows. According to Wikipedia (2014b), the *Hoarders* premiere in 2009 was watched by 2.5 million viewers, 1.8 million of whom were adults aged 18–49. *American Pickers* premiered in 2010 with 3.1 million viewers (Wikipedia, 2014a). The problem with both offering is that they stream sensationalized programming depicting extreme situations into the heads of viewers without thinking of the consequences. Millions of people watching these shows accept what they hear without critical thinking, don't educate themselves on the reality of what they are watching or speak to someone who could provide the answers, and don't consider the source or reasoning behind the programs. They simply agree with what they have watched and heard and accept it as fact. Instead of mandating legal strategies and regularly confronting cultural and social stigmatizations, television programming should move toward telling these stories without completion and leaving them open to reflection and to the collective imagination.

The acts of hoarding, scrounging, and collecting should be viewed through a different lens in light of the massive consumerism in our nation. People discard stuff that seems to have no value but through the right lens the item can gain new value and purpose. Situations and past interactions play out in one person's stuff. Their stuff reflects a larger story of the memories, dramas, and trauma they have endured: life and death, poignant irony and good humor as well. Through the abundance of items and trash, it is difficult to see that most of the items are useful, functional, and desirable objects that many times are unused and new. According to Ferrell (2006):

> The empire features discarded accumulations that cut across an astounding range of consumer choices and disposable lifestyle options, and trash piles into which collapse decades, even centuries, of cultural history—from books and antiques of the 1800s to, quite literally yesterday's purchases.
>
> (p. 45)

A hoarder's home can be seen as an "empire" due to its endless materials that are overwhelming and magnificently chaotic, including mounds of debris. Outsiders think of the home as uninhabitable and dangerous mostly because it is covered throughout with objects. However, hoarders can be viewed as survivalists: people who have been cast out by family members and abandoned by loved ones but still manage to find purpose and value in collecting. Their collections are spewed throughout their homes, designed to make the most of every available corner to stash lost materials given up as trash by previous owners. They find and invent possibilities through their piles of stuff, discovering their true talent, calling, and sense of belonging, even if it is through resistance to societal norms. It is a self-made adventure with its own passion and purpose; collecting stuff leaves them with grins on their faces and wandering eyes for the next treasure, stoking the internal fire of desire and purposeful living. The seductive and alluring items that peek out from boxes and underneath piles keep hoarders enthralled by the discovery of their own possessions, not wanting to discard their glorious trash (that others do not see).

Hoarders tend to operate on their own terms outside of the collective norms of society, usually laughing and enjoying their surroundings until someone finds their lifestyle repulsive and creates havoc by imposing on the hoarders' belief systems about cleanliness. Self-determination and dignity are built out of the piles of items hoarded and reimagined as having purposeful value; however, hoarders internalize shame when onlookers scorn their ideas.

There are, in addition, few differences between hoarders, collectors, and scroungers. All appear to collect things for a lifetime and can tell the story of each item; they have a passion for their collections and believe their items have both personal value as well as worth money. The idea behind collecting, hoarding, and scrounging is to be creative: to create something of value from others' discarded items. People who identify with these activities find value in repurposing an item long discarded. In a country that believes in mass production and mass distribution but also believes equally in environmentally friendly recycling, how can these two processes not coexist to create a resolution? Social and media criticism of hoarding, scrounging, and gleaning reinforce a throwaway culture and complicate progress in reducing trash through repurposing items. The 1987 Mobro garbage barge is a great example of the trash dilemma in our country; it circled the Atlantic waterways for 112 days attempting to negotiate with five states and two foreign countries to dispose of 3,100 tons of trash (Gutis, 1987).

Strasser (1999) also details the New York trash dilemma of 1998 where the Fresh Kills landfill was nearly full and New York attempted to make arrangements to ship their trash to New Jersey but was met with protest. In attempts to secure a contract with the state of Virginia, the New York mayor declared that other states should accept their trash because their state provided cultural benefits for tourists from all over America. His statements were met with more complaints; however, Charles City County (the poorest county in Virginia) operated a 934-acre landfill and they accepted New York's trash for the money to help build schools and cut property taxes (Strasser, 1999, pp. 291–292). Powerful institutions play for high stakes in such debates on trash and consumption, and the prospects are not encouraging, according to Strasser: "People of the developed economies show no sign of giving up their status objects and handy products, nor will those from less developed ones give up their desire for the popular consumer goods of the twentieth century" (p. 292). What an impasse this has left the country at.

Despite the nation's ongoing trash debate, hoarded and reused belongings continue to be viewed in the media and by onlookers as disgusting, worthless, and worthy of landfills. Giroux (2014) makes a valid point when he states that,

> hope, driven by imagination, yearns for more than a retreat into the language of criticism. Hope can energize and mobilize groups, neighborhoods, communities, campuses, and networks of people to articulate and advance insurgent discourses in the movement towards developing an insurrectional democracy.
>
> (pp. 228–229)

Can people's viewpoint on what constitutes trash be changed by educating society on the growing need for repurposing in order to decrease the environmental crisis of too much trash?

Viewing people who collect, hoard, and scrounge through a depth psychological lens shows that they see themselves in the objects collected, feel internal value by finding external value in repurposing items discarded by others, and know they exist and have purpose because of these items. Imagining ways an object can be useful, knowing that someone has not given up on the object and sent it to the landfill, can be mirrored in an image of self as not discarded, abandoned, or purpose-less. This can be a symbolic experience for hoarders that is real and affects them as much as the real event. A hoarder's shadow qualities are lived out through both outer and interior acts, and psyche is not aware of the difference. The shadow is where one can find the pure gold of the personality, according to Johnson (1991), because "it can find no place in that great leveling process that is culture" (p. 7).

4

SEEING THE PERSON IN
THE HOARDER

> Existing comprehensive theories are important not because they are fully developed explanations of human behavior, but because they ask most of the important questions about the subject in a coherent fashion.
>
> (Maddi & Costa, 1972, p. ix)

Articulating general principles that govern behavior, including self-exploration and observation of others, is something many individuals can become proficient in. Someone who had extensive knowledge in this area was trait theorist Henry Murray.

Murray had considerable interest in human traits and characteristics. He received his background training in the medical field, obtaining a medical degree from Columbia in 1919 and then completing a doctorate in biochemistry from Cambridge 9 years later. This set the foundation for his work with Jung. After Murray read one of Jung's books and arranged a meeting with him, Jung encouraged Murray to study psychoanalysis, which he eventually did at Harvard University. With his unique background in both medical and analytical training, Murray focused on the basic need principle in personality, which he called psychogenic needs. He believed these needs were largely at the unconscious level, and he located 27 needs that he believed were influenced and carried out by environmental forces. "He called these forces 'press,' referring to the pressure they put on us that forces us to act'" (AllPsych Online, 2011, p. 2). However, Murray believed there was a difference between real environmental pressures and those that are merely perceived. Murray developed the Thematic Apperception Test (TAT), which measured personality themes as well as unconscious motivations, and has stood up to the research.

According to Murray, in the personalities of all people lie both rational and irrational processes, with a large measure of rationality. With that said, Freudian theory states that human behavior originates in, and is determined largely by, unconscious, inexorable, selfish, primitive impulses. Freud believed ego to be a rational agent. Individuals respond and interact with both external and internal forces where drives are formulated, usually love and death respectively.

> According to this extreme view, whatever rationality man seems to express in thought processes involving planning, decision making, and achieving intellectual understanding is in large measure defensive use of cognition in order to conceal the underlying irrational impulses that are the basic determinants of functioning.
>
> (Maddi & Costa, 1972, p. 25)

For some, irrational unconscious processes can be seen in hoarders as inconsistencies, compulsions, and ego-alien acts.

There is growing interest in applying psychology to the solution of many current social and environmental problems, and those venturesome psychologists who have gone into the field have returned with the news that there is much needed knowledge about human behavior that is hard to deduce either from work in the laboratory or the clinic. (Maddi & Costa, 1972, p. xii)

Murray (1981) states that "personology" is a more accurate term to describe the branch of psychology focusing on the study of human lives and the different aspects that affect their direction; he calls "the psychology of personality" a clumsy and tautological expression (p. 10). He continues by clarifying that personology is psychology; it is what psychology should be about. Murray's mission is clear:

> Personalities constitute the subject matter for psychology, the life history of a single man being a unit with which this discipline has to deal and launches into the most important journey of his intellectual life by providing a new designation for his efforts.
>
> (Murray, 1981, p. 97)

Murry believes that breaking down the structure of each personality into elements and illuminating whatever merit that structure holds should be the task of a psychologist. When reflecting back on how the media and the collective society look at individuals who hoard, scrounge, or glean, the following thought from Murray is eloquent and provoking:

> In our time, the capacities for wonder and reverence, for generous judgments and trustful affirmations, have largely given way, though not without cause surely, to their antitheses, the humors of a waning ethos: disillusionment, cynicism, disgust, and gnawing envy. These states have bred in us the inclination to dissect the subtlest orders of a man's wit with ever sharper instruments of depreciation, to pour all values, the best confounded by the worst, into one mocking-pot to sneer "realistically," and, as we say today, to "assassinate" character.
>
> (Murray, 1981, p. 82)

Whereas Murray pays particular attention to how personality plays out in the development of a person, Hillman focuses on the character of the individual as soul's formative power influences and instigates behavior, patterning movements as an abstraction until it is met with a courageous will to live, its judicious decision, or its humor. In *The Force of Character and the Lasting Life*, Hillman (1999) stated, "We make soul by embodying and enacting adjectives that differentiate the soul's prolific potential. Through these characteristics, we come to know the nature of our soul and can assess the souls of others" (p. 11). The infrastructure of character is built by its qualities, which give it purpose and shape. Having a structured character is not necessarily connected to moral virtues. Staying true to form is a noble endeavor; however, that form may not be strong or true, but rather facile, sneaky, or even corrupt while still forming fate. Hillman imagines a person's psyche to be full of characters—some who show up regularly and follow rules, and others who stay behind closed doors or only come out at night (p. 32).

John Tarrant (1998), in his book *The Light Inside the Dark*, writes that soul and spirit set up house in the place called character, which is a container to endure mortifications needed for growth of awareness and creative work (pp. 171–172). When the container of character is not intact, understanding character through its absence may feel like repetitive pain that seems unnecessary. Hillman (1999) believes that character is concerned with heart failures of love, inner truth, honor, and the suppression of beauty—trying to keep beauty absent so it doesn't attack one's heart and trigger ferocious longings one doesn't know how to appease (p. 122). Again, Tarrant dovetails with Hillman's observation in explaining that setting the container with inner awareness creates the strength by which individuals can hold life, allowing them to have weight, fertility, and endurance (pp. 175–177). In order to face the pain in our lives, it is important to start by looking compassionately and truthfully at our own minds. What types of characters live there? Anger, hate, unforgiveness, loss, loneliness? These characters become the norm of daily life; they are parts of the self that take on shadow qualities that keep an individual stuck in a debilitating disorder.

Like Tarrant, Hillman believes that character endures because it is a weight-bearing structure that individuals feel as a burden. Both Hillman and Tarrant discuss integrity in relationship to character in their respective books. "Integrity does not mean having a granite jaw. A filigree is also a pattern; a house of cards is also a structure" (Hillman, 1999, p. 12). It wants an individual to be what one is, nothing more or other, per Hillman. Tarrant explains that even though there is much invested in one's direction in life, integrity means having the ability to turn about or change course, which he believes is more important than not making mistakes. "Turning about is related to the ability to see the path as something that goes on and on, with infinite vistas. Our faults are always large and visible to all; compassion and perseverance are always necessary" (Tarrant, 1998, p. 201). Individuals have the capacity to separate themselves from old habits and wake up living more consciously. However, staying asleep (avoidance) seems to have a strong pull for individuals. Sitting at a crossroad, individuals continue to struggle with which path to choose: clarity and happiness or confusion and pain.

Hillman goes on to state that each person's fate is plotted and formed by soul's active intelligence, entangling a person's soul, drawing forth their character providing a glimpse into the great myths. Therefore, in order to gain insight into a hoarder's struggles, a sense of myth and knowledge of myths is crucial, because myths show the imaginative structure inside their messes, and the background of the characters of myth can be located in human characters (Hillman, 1999, p. 11).

> "Soul" has become a refuge of mystery and mist, a fairytale land of fantasy and feeling, of dream and reverie, of mood, symbol, and vibrations, a passive loveliness, ungraspable and vulnerable as a butterfly's wing. The idea of form gives shape and character to soul and demands more rigor in thinking about it.
>
> (Hillman, 1999, p. 11)

As this book will show in Chapters 7 and 8, being able to study an individual's personality (or a personology study) and character helps focus on important unresolved issues including the impact of early experiences on personality development, changes in the stability of personality over time, and character and temperament in contrast to situation in forecasting behavioral outcomes (Alexander, 1990, p. 10). Being able to describe referential points in time from childhood, adolescence, and old age to show consistencies over the life span, and also linking outcomes and the factors that influenced them, are crucial in understanding an individual's hoarding dynamic. Being able to extract and retain what is critical or uncover something crucial to the pathology of an individual suffering with hoarding tendencies is imperative to achieve overall recovery and growth. Irving E. Alexander (1990), a clinical psychologist and cofounder of the Society for Personology, stated that extracting the salient aspects of an individual's psychobiography and factoring them into common or unique sequential patterns allowed for effective processing of the data, uncovering dimensions of the individual not previously seen (p. 52).

This process speaks to the nature of understanding hoarding from another dimension outside of the clinical model. To understand hoarding tendencies, one must look past the symptomology and into the mystery of the behaviors of those trapped within their clutter. Murray and Hillman would concur that before any intervention can be applied with hoarders, it is important to learn more about how they see themselves, their options, and the environmental forces impinging upon them.

The modern worldview has assigned great importance to individualism, an ideal that has too often been degraded into a self-indulgent, egoistic, and aggressive quest for power and material gain (Schlitz, Amorok, & Micozzi, 2005, p. 11). For a healer, intensely personal inner work is needed and should be ongoing throughout one's lifetime. The goal of a healer's work is love and acceptance of self, which then allows for love and acceptance of others. Possessing an intact self for a healer can then promote the healing of another. According to William Benda in his excerpt entitled *From Integrative to Integral Medicine: A Leap of Faith*, "when the intent to heal another comes from our place of inner knowing, we instinctively and automatically know what to do" (cited in Schlitz *et al.*, 2005, p. 36). Benda continues to maintain that what matters most is what is best for the patient, not a desire for financial gain, position, or power. Maintaining the patient's trust is central to the therapy process, especially when difficult decisions need to be made for their welfare. As a healer, equality and social justice are paramount to the therapeutic process and just as equal is allowing the patient to be the master of his or her body, mind, and soul- surrendering control as a healer, allowing the outcome to blossom into a sense of empowerment (Benda, cited in Schlitz *et al.*, 2005, p. 37).

In order to exercise a more complete approach with patients, the importance of the therapeutic encounter between therapist and patient is vital. Patients must be allowed autonomy in therapy through informed options, placing the therapist in the sharing position and not the hierarchy/dictating position. The optimal therapeutic situation occurs when the therapist employs an individual treatment plan utilizing all modalities, conventional and alternative, that is tailored specifically to the patient's needs where both can recognize the innate healing properties of the human body conducive to a healthy recovery (Benda, cited in Schlitz *et al.*, 2005, p. 34).

> As I see it, a psychologist should be concerned not only with the formulation of overt interpersonal verbal communications, the immediate (intended) effects of which are changes of some kind among the dispositions, evaluations, represented facts, interpretations, or commitments of the other person, but also with the formulation of covert introverted mental activities, the immediate (intended) effects of which are such things as: a better interpretation and explanation of some recalled event or of some current physical symptoms, a re-evaluation of one's own enactions (past behaviors) or present abilities, the definition of the content and boundaries of a required concept, the composition of the plot of a story to be written, the resolution of a conflict between two purposes, or the ordination of a plan of action (tactics) to be executed at some future date.
>
> (Murray, 1981, p. 20)

Murray's and Hillman's beliefs on how psychologists should practice raise the question: how can a discipline that honors individual human behavior not spend considerable time studying and theorizing about the behavior of humans over their life span in their natural social and physical environments, taking into account their needs, options, and limitations? "Almost no one (other than anthropologists whose interests are not primarily psychological) takes any systematic account of what people do when freely behaving, what they have to say about their experience, and how they explain their behavior" (Maddi & Costa, 1972, p. x). Therefore, it is imperative that personologists focus on the macro events, or *proceedings*, as Murray would call them, to extract relevant variables like need, entity, configuration, process, succession, effect, place, route, and time that correspond to their purpose.

Americans are receptive to factual information that leads to a diagnosis and treatment, but the pragmatism and objectivity in which they intellectually take pride can also create vulnerability to accepting answers that there are no valid questions. Consequently, and in line with Murray, Alexander (1990) makes a controversial point in his book *Personology* when he states, "The study of a life lived is more likely to call attention to the explanation of those aspects of the life history which do not seem to flow easily from either common sense or simple psychological principles" (p. 9). To the inexperienced onlooker, who hoarders were and how they got this way may not be obvious. There is a curious fascination with those who have an abnormal condition.

5

TURNING A DIAGNOSIS INTO SOUL WORK

Hoarding behavior may be a disorder in its own category, with distress and dysfunction as determining factors. Distinguishing hoarding from other anxiety and mood disorders is difficult because hoarders tend to be ashamed of their disorder and standoffish or unreceptive to those who would impede their activities. Hoarders are both intimate with and embarrassed by the same matter, creating the tension of the opposites—a double life with their interaction with their objects. The two most common reactions associated with people who hoard are shame, due to the excess amount of clutter, and a surprising lack of awareness of just how severe the problem is. According to Tolin *et al.* (2007), the person might sometimes acknowledge that there is a problem, but at other times he or she asserts that nothing is wrong (p. 17).

The origins of compulsive behaviors in individuals are just as challenging to pinpoint, resulting in diagnosis and treatment of this population being challenging.

> The clues to why people hoard are not so simple or straightforward to decipher but may be discovered in the complex interaction of personality and circumstances, in an individual's ability to respond to life events in a certain way, in genetics, or in more serious psychiatric issues that manifest themselves in classic hoarding behaviors.
>
> (Paxton, 2011, p. 38)

A study conducted by Frost, Kyrios, McCarthy, and Matthews (2007) supported the hypothesis that self-ambivalence and uncertainty about self and others are associated with measures of compulsive hoarding and the notion that acquiring and accumulating objects may constitute attempts to bolster one's certainty about self-worth and engender a sense of security (pp. 239–240).

Hoarding has been continually studied from a clinical standpoint as a problem of emotional, mental, behavioral, and social well-being. "What we do mean is that people with compulsive hoarding are not fully in control of their behaviors. They are hooked into a pattern of behavior that even they cannot fully understand or manage" (Tolin *et al.*, 2007, p. 29). The way people act, feel, and think are how they relate to their possessions. Furthermore, their thinking and beliefs can become so rigid and intense, so strong and inflexible, that they create insurmountable roadblocks in reducing clutter. James Hollis (1998) mirrors this clinical standpoint from a depth perspective in his book *The Eden Project*. He states that soul demands growth but is stifled when a person falls in love with love. He cites Dante, saying that the worst inferno is becoming overtaken by what a person seeks. A person longs to die in the other, like an addict, and to be subsumed until the desired object holds the person captive (Hollis, 1998, p. 61). Hollis further states that psyche knows what is right for us and what is developmentally demanded. "When we use the Other [objects] to avoid our own task, we may be able to fool ourselves for a while, but the soul will not be mocked" (p. 80). The soul wishes its fullest expression; therefore, psyche will express its protest through activated complexes.

People who hoard frequently report feeling violated, as if they are losing parts of themselves or their identity, in the process of ridding their homes of possessions (Frost & Hartl, 1996; Steketee, Frost, & Kyrios, 2003). They may also conceivably feel that they have violated others by getting rid of items once owned by loved ones.

> The intensity of this reaction is out of line with the extent to which the possession is needed for any instrumental reason and excessive compared to comparable experiences of people without hoarding problems. It appears as though owning the possession, rather than using it, is integral to the hoarder's sense of self.
>
> (Frost *et al.*, 2007, p. 234)

When the disorder is examined on the surface level, treating just the compulsion and anxiety associated with hoarding, individuals respond by doing things that are self-damaging: acting stubborn, digging in their heels, and resisting making changes. The complex human condition of hoarding can fall victim to normativism when researchers employ theories that set out to explain the disorder from the ego function and ego's tendency towards reductionism. Pain and one-sidedness are the results of reductionism, which cuts out the vastness of the psyche, creating a loss of soul. Psyche's mysterious qualities lie in how it lives in the facts of things and is also the spirit of things. "We all have to be so careful with all theories, for they are only as good as they are helpful to living with the mysteries and discovering rich human lives" (Wikman, 2004, p. 254). It is vital to pay attention to the nuances of an experience in the psyche, without reductionism, in order to endure the heat of the opposites: guilt, shame, and loss. The practice of psychology inherently endangers people who hoard when it tries to force normative ideas onto their lives and their illness.

Marie Von Franz (1980) wrote that to get to the bottom of someone's problem, it is necessary first to find the makeup of such drives: "We all have them in us and until we bring them up and face them we have a hidden corner where they live autonomously" (p. 127). Hollis (1998) asked a pertinent question that is central to uncovering the drives of a person with uncontrollable acquisition problems: "How many have lived their whole lives shrouded in guilt and repression for the merest manifestation of the natural desires of their own soul?" (p. 100). The unconscious is where such drives reside. That said, people's conscious and unconscious beliefs about independence and autonomy hinder their decisions about discarding, saving, and acquiring clutter. "The emotional security associated with the possessions may further compensate for the lack of emotional rewards, giving a sense of security about the world around them and about their own esteem" (Frost *et al.*, 2007, p. 235).

A hoarder's complexes and triggers, which are mostly unconscious, can unleash powerful urges to acquire that to others seem illogical. Hillman (1983b) stated that complexes can't be found by just letting go, and that they don't respond to worry, searching parties, or naturalists with tags and labels: "The complexes in the deep have their own body and their own will, and this is not bound to the ego's bylaws of compensation" (p. 59). Jacobi (1959) further stated that "complexes have not only an obsessive, but often a possessive character, behaving like imps and giving rise to all sorts of annoying, ridiculous, and revealing actions, slips of the tongue, and falsifications of memory and judgment" (p. ix). For this reason, the *story* that a hoarder creates when in deep depression, although it may or may not have occurred, subsequently creates a "real" trigger that begins the hoarding: "It's very tempting for hoarders to avoid the realities completely and focus instead on a fantasy" (Paxton, 2011, p. 43). The fear of the story itself for a hoarder allows for repression to be built into the story or the fantasy made material in the hoarded possessions. "I need to remember my stories not because I need to find out about myself but because I need to found myself in a story I can hold to be 'mine'" (Hillman, 1983b, p. 42). Having a story through identification with their possessions allows individuals who hoard to experience feelings of being needed or valued. They link their possessions to their sense of self, creating a life based on objects possessed instead of actual living. Hoarders describe their objects as an extension of themselves and say that losing an object would be like losing a particular day in their life (Frost & Steketee, 2010, p. 116).

One example of this is the "hunt and gather" experience for hoarders. This experience is a primal rush for hoarders and helps them avoid the conscious reality of their complexes. The pleasure derived from shopping (hunting) and acquiring (gathering) is so intense and overwhelmingly rewarding for a person who hoards that it erases all thoughts of consequences or rationality. Some individuals have described this phenomenon as being "in the zone," describing dissociative-like states where they become so focused on the hunting and gathering (i.e. purchasing) that they forget about the context of their lives, including whether they have the money, space, or need for the object (Frost & Steketee, 2010, p. 70). Every personal object in hoarders' territory has special meaning and becomes part of their personas, both positive and negative. The embodied selves of hoarders can be seen in the images of their stashes as putrid and dark. Susan Lepselter (2011) makes the correlation between the disordered embodiment and the "deep meanings of accumulated possessions that are affectively and imaginatively tied to private meanings of the past, as memory, and to the future, as desire and potential" (p. 926).

A hoarder's motivation for saving items is to create a private identity and not a public one. Many hoarders see value in things no one else wants, mirroring their own discarded selves and the potential that no one else may see. "The great limitation of ego consciousness is that it tends to concretize reality in order to make itself feel secure about its own place in the scheme of things" (Woodman & Dickson, 1996, p. 67). Woodman and Dickson state further that ego consciousness perceives life in terms of doing, and doing implies being able to control and manipulate, allowing one to think life is safe and secure (p. 67). However, in doing this, hoarders seek an impossible ideal, failing to live and slowly killing themselves day by day with their excessive clutter.

"We must become aware that though we thirst for love, we yet reject it because we fear it, and so take refuge in the flat banality of daily life" (Carotenuto, 1989, p. 17). Carotenuto writes that love makes lone wolves of us because we are less in tune with others and less able to communicate our experience (p. 17); he further elaborates that love then is seen as a generator of images, of daemons, who with their explosive power alter or destroy all sense of proportion and balance (p. 19). Hoarding behaviors can be seen as experiences in which something else becomes the source of the hoarders' ecstasy, their happiness depending upon objects, at the mercy of the fantasy created. The loss and vulnerability that hoarders experience in relation to the objects they acquire can be seen as conditions of the soul. They long to be loved, accepted, and nurtured, accepting even the mirror projection of their soul back to them from their objects. Objects to a hoarder can be perceived as loving them unconditionally especially in an environment where others have failed them.

"When there is too big a gap between our 'wishful' image and our true self, we will be constantly troubled by anxiety because we fear that others will see through us" (Au & Cannon, 1995, p. 25). Adult disapproval and punishment caused us to repress or hide parts of ourselves that were deemed "ugly." They were repressed into the shadow, an inferior subpersonality that has a life of its own with values and goals contradictory to those we consciously hold. When hoarders use their objects as a way to avoid the task of working through their complexes, soul will protest. "Depression, chronic anxiety, and various forms of physical illness and addictions are also ways in which the psyche can express unconscious conflicts and signal the need for honest self-confrontation" (Au & Cannon, 1995, p. 19). Unless hoarders do conscious work on unveiling their repressed darkness, their shadow is projected and directed toward someone or placed on something so they don't have to accept responsibility for it. Again, as previously stated, an individual's repressed feelings of shame, his or her shadow material, become unconsciously projected into their clutter, veiling it from existence.

There is no growth without suffering, and experiencing suffering through the encounter with the shadow can facilitate movement into areas of their lives where people would not ordinarily go. All psychological progress is blocked without the realization of one's own shadow. Jung emphasized this by saying, "*One cannot avoid the shadow* [Jung's emphasis] unless one remains neurotic, and as long as one is neurotic one has omitted the shadow" (Jung, 1946/1960, p. 545). Hoarders, like most human beings, hunger for wholeness: harmony, contentment, and peace. Knowing what wholeness is can be felt by experiencing their shadow and its conflict. Confrontation of one's own motivations and attitudes, which lurk in the shadow, is necessary to achieve wholeness.

The beginning of self-knowledge is understanding something about one's own shadow side. Hoarders are overwhelmed by alienation as their relationships fall apart. They fear aloneness, separateness from the Other, and deadness of the soul. Hoarders feel unstable as the ground beneath them becomes shaky. They attempt to grab onto anything or anyone to alleviate their suffering, living consciously, trying to exert control through the chaos. People who hoard deceive themselves into believing they have control, trying to push down their shadow material from rising into consciousness, fearing what it might reveal. Wearing masks, they wander through their day with a pretense of humanity, only to go back to the madness of their setting that will provide temporary peace and safety. "In other words, life has not lived in the body; the soul has not taken up residence" (Woodman & Dickson, 1996, p. 173).

Avoiders of conflict believe, "If I ignore something, I can pretend it doesn't exist." However, ignoring shadow material out of fear of what they might discover or postponing the inner work of self only allows the energies of the shadow to intensify over time and with age. "But the refused and unacceptable characteristics do not go away; they only collect in the dark corners of our personality" (Johnson, 1991, p. 4).

"When we seek happiness through accumulation, either outside of ourselves— from other people, relationships, or material goods—or from our own self- development, we are missing the essential point" (Epstein, 1998, p. xviii). In *Going to Pieces without Falling Apart*, Epstein states that we are trying to locate completion, which does not come from adding other pieces to ourselves. Completion is found when we surrender our ideals of perfectionism. By pushing ourselves further into the unknown, we can achieve a sense of feeling more real. Epstein also indicates that in order to feel whole, one must touch the ground of emptiness. By not rushing to change to our feelings of emptiness but just being with them, we can access the still, silent center of awareness that has been hiding behind the veil of shame and embarrassment (Epstein, 1998, pp. 26–27). Epstein asserts that this is why we shy away from intimacy; it puts us in touch with our own vulnerability and fragility, and instead of learning how to be tolerant of these difficult emotions, we avoid them.

We spend a lot of time cut off from our own bodies, accumulating physical and emotional tension, sometimes outside of our awareness, nursing a grievance or two. Delusions, motivated by fear and insecurities, creep into our minds, and we seek premature closure by imposing boundaries to wall ourselves off and find safety (Epstein, 1998, p. 126). How does one nurture a stronger self of self? Epstein (1998) states that mindfulness of body and feelings allows individuals to get to know themselves again by experiencing both pleasant and unpleasant sensations (pp. 106–107). Epstein concludes by stating:

> In building a path through the self to the far shore of awareness, we have to carefully pick our way through our own wilderness. We do not have to break our way through as much as we have to find our way around the major obstacles. We do not have to cure every neurosis, we just have to learn how not to be caught by them.
>
> (p. 119)

Learning to let go allows happiness room to grow and flourish.

The shadow life consists of all the unwanted or repressed sides of ourselves that have been hidden long enough, and they eventually take on a life all their own. Unless hoarders do conscious work on unveiling their repressed darkness, their shadow is projected—directed toward someone or placed on something so they don't have to accept responsibility for it. Jung expressed this idea further by writing in 1949, "No one stands beyond good and evil, otherwise he would be out of this world. Life is a continual balancing of opposites, like every other energic process. The abolition of opposites would be equivalent to death" (Jung, 1973, p. 16). Perhaps there is a side of the shadow that hoarders are afraid to identify with even though their shadow can be comprised of the best of them—the tension of the opposites, both positive and negatives. Integration of both, shadow and light, is needed for wholeness.

6

ATTENDING TO THE VOICES OF HOARDERS

The six individual voices in the following chapter were selected because they present an opportunity to view the disorder of hoarding from the collective perspective and through the eyes of the individual psyche. The words metaphorically heard through each of their voices are the call of psyche through language, supporting understanding and providing an interaction between the disorder and the individual. Providing an accurate dialogue of their lives and truthfulness to their stories was imperative to understand how this disorder seeped into their lives and interwove itself into their dwellings and souls. "A work of literature is not an object we understand by conceptualizing or analyzing it; it is a voice we must hear, and through 'hearing' (rather than seeing) understand" (Palmer, 1969, p. 11).

While reading the stories of the six individuals in the following chapter, the challenge is to read with fluidity and openness. The goal is to take the life stories of these individuals from analysis to translation and bringing what is obscure and clinical in its meaning into something meaningful that speaks from a soul language. Hoping for nothing and being patient with no expectation to fix or treat them but a desire to question their processes, which then will provide the right space for a hoarder to experience the numinous with his or her hoarded objects. In his book *Truth and Method*, Hans-Georg Gadamer (1975) detailed an approach that would allow such a dynamic to happen. He believed a text bestowed upon the reader its procedure or method and allowed for clarification upon which understanding takes place—placing the reader in the receiving position, not the driving force through prejudices.

> In fact our own prejudice is properly brought into play by being put at risk. Only by being given full play is it able to experience the other's claim to truth and make it possible for him to have full play himself.
>
> (Gadamer, 1975, p. 299)

By implementing this type of reading style, Palmer (1969) believes a reader can be sensitive to the experience of understanding what is being written and experience the reading without translating from the shallow place of knowledge, but rather from a "loving union" between text and interpreter—partners in the hermeneutic dialogue (p. 244). Allowing the words to tell the reader something and assert their own truth is the goal of this type of reading experience, and this can only be achieved if readers are aware of their own bias. What is largely missing from a clinical approach to literature is a meaningful encounter with it—being seized by the words written. Palmer (1969) asserts that "the text must be allowed to speak, the reader being open to it as a subject in its own right rather than as an object" (p. 197). Distinguishing between opinion and truth in what is written is achieved through being aware of one's bias and discarding prejudices.

According to Gadamer (1975), "this openness always includes our situating the other meaning in relation to the whole of our own meanings or ourselves in relation to it" (p. 271). An abundance of possibilities will flow from meaning. However, projection is problematic when reading the written word. As soon as a meaning for the written word emerges a projection can be made by the reader for the story as a whole. This is accomplished by the reader having a particular expectation for the story being read, which allows for the initial meaning to emerge. The task of understanding is accomplished through working out the reader's projections. Remaining open to the meaning of the following stories presented is the essential task placed before the reader. The key is to listen to its voice; a *hearing* understanding allows for meaning to be brought forth. What has been written must be given permission to speak. It should be heard by a great listener with no expectation, judgment, or prejudice.

Being able to read their life stories by honoring fluidity, seeking an understanding from the language of images, metaphors, myths, and symbols in the following chapter allows the voice of their stories to reveal itself. One can only achieve this by employing an imaginal perspective to read the following stories. Robert Romanyshyn (2002) stated in his book *Ways of the Heart*, "I am for better or worse a witness for what has been lost, forgotten, left behind, or otherwise marginalized and neglected, a witness for those lost things which still remain and haunt the outer margins of the experienced world" (p. 113). A witness begins without judgment about the truth or falsity of an experience and with an invitation, a spirit of loving wonderment and generosity. This allows the experience and things to be what they are—as they are (Romanyshyn, 2002, p. 116). It is paramount to experience the setting of a person who hoards from an open, non-judgmental perspective, with curiosity into the imaginal aspects of the objects collected and no need to diagnose or treat.

In *Re-Visioning Psychology*, Hillman (1975) distinguished between ego-based problems and fantasy when approaching a client's problem: "Where problems call for will power, fantasies evoke the power of the imagination. Those who work professionally with imagination recognize the value of fantasies and resist having them turned into psychological problems to be analyzed." (p. 135). Pathologizing is at work when symptomatic events are ignored and ritualized, creating odd behaviors, something symbolic beyond itself.

> The psyche wants to find itself by seeing through; even more, it loves to be enlightened by seeing through itself, as if the very act of seeing-through clarified and made transparent—as if psychologizing with ideas were itself an archetypal therapy, enlightening, illuminating.
>
> (Hillman, 1975, p. 123)

When the soul is overwhelmed by events, it suffers. By implementing fantasy and evoking the power of imagination, problems are dissolved and not analyzed, and psychologizing can solve the matter at hand with visibility and light. Hillman (1975) stated, "Fantasy need not always be verbal, nor must there be a visual imagery" (p. 143). He believes that by entering into a more skilled way of doing things, one can translate an event into an experience through style, gesture, or ritual, allowing for psychologizing to break up the repetitiveness of clinical treatment and diagnosis. Soul is obstructed by the literalism, methods, and tools of psychology, and the more a psychology is backed by hard evidence, the less open soul becomes in releasing insight due to the production of a single definition instead of multiple ambiguities of meaning.

We must seek an ensouled language with the stories in the next chapter, including heartfelt images and symbols placed upon objects hoarded, increasing our conscious beliefs enough to encompass both subtle and explicit energies through recognition from dreams, visions, reverie, and the collective.

> Too what is implied here is that we cannot solve the pathologies of our-selves or our patients, or our environmental problems, by the use of scientific terminology and theoretical formulations alone (such as have been developed in empirical epistemologies), for these, though easier, are inadequate to the task of transformation.
>
> (Goodchild, 2001, p. 174)

Changing from a discipline of psychology to a more activity-based psycho-therapy is imperative in releasing the dynamic energies of psyche (the unconscious) and soul (the embodied spirit), both different from each other. Fantasy and afflictions are expressed by psyche in the mode of symptoms; however, a distinct entity is produced with literal reality when symptoms are professionally named by psychology, creating protection and separation from this named entity. "By taking soul's sickness fantasy at face values clinical pathology, the clinical approach creates what it then must treat" (Hillman, 1975, p. 74). Having room for the bizarre, decayed, and fantastic in the objects and settings of a hoarder allows for therapy to follow this peculiar disorder, letting it be our guide to the ways of psyche and finding soul. Returning to the understanding of the nosology of disorder as diagnosis to the material disorder of the soul hidden in the hoard is imperative to the research. It must stay connected to the poetics of hoarding, in the sense that the hoarder is in the process of making some meaning from and out of the mess—open and porous to the images that gather in what their hoarding wants to say.

By abandoning the medical model, we can stay connected to the mess, allowing soul to lead therapists into the madness created by a hoarder's imagination. Metaphor is the language of the soul; soul has no language and therefore speaks in imagery. Romanyshyn (2002) accentuates this statement further by stating, "We live in dark times because we have largely lost our capacity for an imaginal way of knowing and being and have largely forgotten how to appreciate the imaginal depths of the world" (p. 116). Soul communicates eternal truths to beings both eternal and temporal, a metaphorical language that current psychology ignores. What is life if not lived through imagination and imagery? According to Woodman and Dickson (1996), without this connection to soul, shorter and fewer workdays, unemployment, and boredom can trap exiled souls in the demonic version of an archetypal madman or madwoman who promises superhuman light on one side, superhuman sex on the other, with no room for human life in the middle (p. 186). Culture, dreams, symptoms, and religion become meaningless. Life becomes one-dimensional, flat, boring, and intolerable. Metaphors act as guides and imagination moves ahead, beneath, around, and through the action. By this I mean that soul needs to dance with imagination.

As Romanyshyn (2002) so eloquently stated, "a mode of being in the world that is responsive to the luminosity in each moment, the shining radiance of the invisible that subtends the visible" (p. 165). Romanyshyn echoed Hillman (1981): "imagination begins in a heart aware that there is both true and false imagining and that these are not contradictories, but rather correlatives, even co-terminous" (p. 73). The sophistication of its imaginings begins with the heart's illusions. If we engage the heart, we can move into imagination. "For when the brain is considered to be the seat of consciousness we search for literal locations, whereas we cannot take the heart with the same physiological literalism" (Hillman, 1981, p. 109). Leading with heart allows for a loving presence amid the clutter while it leaves judgment at the front door.

Science was founded by a claim of legitimacy through objectivity; however, today it seems more like a fallacy than truth. The credibility of objectivity is an issue, allowing projections to enter the therapeutic experience where we are left with subjectivity.

Science today cannot but acknowledge that objectivity, the most cherished of its ideals, is unattainable. The experimenter cannot detach herself from her experiments; the thinker cannot separate himself from his thoughts. The observer is as much a participant in an event as the observed. (Woodman & Dickson, 1996, p. 217)

While reading the following chapter, nothing should be taken literally or at face value; a deeper kind of inquiry needs to be at work. "Imagination is the key to the work, to the inner garden, to the intermediate realm of symbol that moves and changes us and our lives as it shows how to unite the opposites" (Wikman,

2004, p. 224). Being conscious of our standpoint (biases, vulnerabilities, and ways of connecting and dialoguing with psyche) is paramount to imagination and the process of incarnating the latent self. Hillman (1983b) eloquently stated that it is the imagination that allows us to see *events as images* by giving them distance and dignity (p. 45). By allowing for objects, settings, and individuals to be seen through their symptoms, symbols, dreams, and fantasies, the reader can be open to other alternative meanings, not just diagnostically. Seeing through a lens of inquiry illuminates respect for and attention to the true complexity of an experience adding depth and mystery to their stories. "One must remain continually aware of unawareness, keeping an eye and an ear for the opposite, the other thing" (Von Franz, 1980, p. 144).

Activating soul, spirit, and psyche are fundamental in understanding the condition of hoarding from a depth psychological perspective. "A depth psychologist functions, in part, like a naturalist, appreciating and investigating the vast wilderness of being and not co-opting the terrain or manipulating it with too much theory or fixed thought forms" (Wikman, 2004, p. 125). By offering this type of approach to the stories presented in the next chapter it allows for soul to be engaged and a willingness to invite the imaginal in while viewing the landscape of a hoarder's home—a way of deepening the event into an experience.

Proceeding into the following chapter, it is important not to link one individual's imagery experience of an object with all individuals who hoard that particular object. It is imperative not to create a bias toward an individual story based on a highlighted dramatic experience or link it to others who have suffered the same type of experiences, thereby creating a fixed set of images for objects. We as readers need to allow each individual's stories and objects hoarded to speak for themselves. When individuals verbalize emotional, psychological, physical, and social difficulties, their experiences should not be viewed as collective experiences for all hoarders. Coppin and Nelson (2005) solidify this ethical consideration: "It is essential to inquire of any event, person, dream, emotion, image, mood, thought, insight or fascination" and repeat the important idea that "all things, every object and every action, take on significance to soul" (p. 91). It is essential when reading the next chapter to allow soul to speak for itself, without bias, judgment, or criticism, and to be heard by all ears willing to listen with an openness to and respect for the imaginal.

What follows is a summary of each person's demographic profile and an overview of their family lineage, as well as a detailed description of each person's hoarding setting and objects hoarded. The most notably recognized hoarders in history were chosen for the study, including a mother and daughter, two brothers, an individual woman, and another individual man. These individuals were selected due to the considerable amount of biological background information available and the descriptions of their hoarding settings and objects hoarded. Being able to assess a person's disorder depends on gathering all available information in order to provide a meaningful evaluation; for this reason, some individuals were not chosen due to their limited historical data or an incomplete profile of their hoarding setting.

The material was gathered from a position of not knowing. The participants were not chosen all at once, but one at a time, engaging actively with one figure in order to be fully present with their experience as much as possible. There was no road map on where their stories or experience would lead, but with hope that their stories would reveal commonalities in the extensive background material received on each historical figure. By seeking fluidity and openness, space was made for the unknown, allowing metaphors and images to speak and uncovering what was embedded and hidden in the clutter. These are their stories.

7

PERSONAL STORIES OF HOARDERS

Edith and Edie Beale: Grey Gardens

Dead vines covered the entire front of the 28-room mansion inhabited by 330 cats, numerous raccoons, and a mother and daughter, Edith and Edie Beale. As we journey into the history of these seemingly privileged socialites, we uncover the loss and disappointments that were masked by a mansion of life, frivolity, and grand décor, a journey that transformed the mansion into Grey Gardens, a hoarded home, and two women into hoarders.

> At Grey Gardens the world cannot intrude. I feel it to be as safe and private as any mountain peak in ancient Tibet. With no formality of conduct, convention, or customs, the old house slowly envelops my mind and soul like a soft cocoon.
>
> (Wright, 1978, p. 1)

On this journey of being present with the Beales' lives, 4 months was spent in the company of the material that told their story. I spent 12 weeks reading biographies from people remembering both their lives, gazing at photos that captured a single moment, reading materials handwritten by Little Edie, viewing documentaries filmed by curious onlookers, and sitting with my own imagination, as the researcher of this material, allowing the information to play like a motion picture on the big screen.

According to *Biography*, Edith Ewing Beale (Big Edie) was born on October 5, 1895, to wealthy parents John Vernou Bouvier Jr. and Maude. She was one of five children (A+E Television Networks, 2013b). Her father John was a successful attorney and judge with his own law firm, and her mother was the daughter of a wealthy pulp merchant and paper producer. One of Edith's brothers was John "Black Jack" Vernou Bouvier III, the father of Jacqueline Kennedy Onassis (A+E

Television Networks, 2013b). Previous records show that the Bouviers arrived on American soil without any money, refugees of Napoleon's 1815 tragedy at Waterloo. According to Bouvier Beale Jr. in the book *Edith Bouvier Beale of Grey Gardens: A Life in Pictures*, "Raising itself up on pure guts and gumption, my family became a leading player on Wall Street during the economic boom of the first part of the century" (Beale, 2009, p. 8).

Edith's early years were spent in privileged high society; she lived in a 24-room mansion on Park Avenue in Manhattan with her family. By the age of 10, she was considered by many to be a prodigy at singing and playing the piano, gifts her father considered a waste of time. However, she was trained by the best teachers that money could afford; she sang classical opera beautifully and was among the artistic elite in the 1920s and 1930s (A+E Television Networks, 2013b).

At the age of 22, Edith married Phelan Beale, a man very much like her father. Phelan was an attorney as well, and later made partner in John Bouvier's law firm. The couple frequented the same high society circles that Edith had as a child, and her husband, like her father, felt that Edith's musical aspirations were a waste of her time. Edith and Phelan had three children: Edie, Phelan Jr., and Bouvier. Shortly after the children were born, the couple purchased a 28-room house with ocean views, nicknamed Grey Gardens (A+E Television Networks, 2013b).

During their marriage, Edith preferred to stay home and orchestrate her own lavish parties, where she could sing and play the piano for her guests. Such activity was in contrast to the lifestyle Phelan wanted for them. When they did venture out to cocktail parties, Edith was known for wearing sweaters over her evening gowns and talking about Christian Science, which displeased her family greatly (A+E Television Networks, 2013b). Her grandsons lovingly referred to Edith as "the original bohemian" and described her as a free spirit or an artiste. Some have also stated that Edith was theatrical, self-indulgent, and impractical (Beale, 2009, p. 8).

Her daughter Edie (known as Little Edie) seemed to be a mirror image of Edith as a child. According to A+E Television Networks (2013c), Edie was born on November 7, 1917, during the first year of her parents' marriage. Like her mother, Edie possessed a creative side. She verbalized artistic yearnings and enjoyed singing and modeling. Her real passion was for the stage, but Edie's father objected and attempted to curve her dreams into other avenues. At the age of 9, Edie loved writing poetry, and one of her poems was published in a local New York magazine, fueling her desire to be a part of the New York social scene (A+E Television Networks, 2013c).

According to their biography, when Edie was 11, her mother removed her from school for 2 years due to what she called acute respiratory illness. During that time, Edie lived a life of privilege with daily shopping trips, first-run movies and the theater, luncheons with friends, and lavish vacations. "Filled with family vacations, costume parties, soirees, fashion shows, fundraising functions, and weekly trips to the cinema, the Beale family lived a remarkably loving life within the Hamptons' high society of the early twentieth century" (Beale, 2009, p. 192). During this time period, Edie kept a journal (later published as a book called *I Only Mark the Hours that Shine*), where she detailed her life at the age of 11 as her mother's sidekick, the marital dissatisfaction she witnessed between her parents, and her father's family absences and drinking problem. In her diary entries from January 11–12, 1929, she wrote that as she was heading to bed on Friday her dad stumbled in drunk. That Saturday he was to take them to the movies, but at the last moment he did not show up (Beale, 2010, pp. 8–9). During this time, Edie also started to question her future as well as her desire to pull away from the mainstream expectations of marriage and children. On July 21, 1929, she wrote:

> Have I really got the brains enough to get away from marriage and children? I should like to start out as a chorus girl on the stage—or dance in a nightclub—anything different from the usual routine in life. Perhaps a career on the stage, then have a small apartment and write a few books.
>
> (p. 106)

In the HBO film *Grey Gardens*, directed by Michael Sucsy (2009), Edie is seen running away from her coming-out party out of rebellion against getting married and becoming a wife. She concedes to her mother's famous words, "You can have your cake and eat it too," in reference to marriage and acting.

As a teenager, Edie's life continued to catapult her into the limelight as an actress and model. When she was 17 years old she began modeling for Macy's, earned the nickname "Body Beautiful," and was considered more striking than her cousin Jacqueline Onassis (A+E Television Networks, 2013c). When she moved out of her parents' home, she resided at the Barbizon Hotel in New York, known to house aspiring models and actresses. "During the thirties, in and around the Maidstone Club in East Hampton, Edie was the local fashion model of choice for all of the fund-raisers, women's clubs, or other civic or social events" (Beale, 2009, p. 9). Edie described this as a time of opportunity and mentioned receiving offers for movies from MGM and Paramount studios (A+E Television Networks, 2013c).

During this time, Edie dated Howard Hughes (aviator and film producer) and turned down marriage proposals from Joe Kennedy Jr. (John Kennedy's oldest brother) and millionaire J. Paul Getty (A+E Television Networks, 2013c). However, Edie's mother scared off many suitors interested in her daughter, out of fear she would be left alone with no one to care for her. Even though Edie never married, her true love was Julius Krug, former Secretary of the Interior and a married man. He ended their relationship soon after it began. In the HBO film, Edie states, "What we had was special," but he states, "What we had was just sex" (Sucsy, 2009). Edie was broken-hearted.

Edie also suffered another loss: the loss of her hair. She contracted alopecia in her 20s, which rendered her bald. Edie used unique wraps to cover her hair loss, including scarves, towels, and shirts, as depicted in both films and photographs.

Peter Beard, a famous photographer who visited Grey Gardens in 1972, described the setting as "animals, fur collared costumes, songs at the drop of a hat, dramatic performances/monologues spilling over with dreams (mostly fantasies)— some sad, often heroic—life enhancing dreams with family history—20's and 30's paintings leaning against the walls" (Beale, 2009, p. 7). Additionally, he describes the environment with the two Beales as never a dull moment, new, insanely funny, poignant, wild, unpredictable and unmatchable both afternoon and evenings (p. 7). However, as time passed, the environment Edith and Edie inhabited changed, their disposition and behavior began transforming to mirror the deterioration of the home that encapsulated them.

By the mid-1930s, Phelan left Edith for a younger woman but later divorced her. Grey Gardens and child support were all Edith received for compensation from the marriage. Edith contacted her father John for financial support and also sold off heirlooms. Edie was around 19 years old when her parents divorced but continued to follow her dreams in New York, checking on her mother regularly (A+E Television Networks, 2013b).

At the same time, Edith's dreams of being a singer soared, so that she distanced herself from the socialite scene. She began to frequent nightclubs to showcase her talent and even recorded a few songs. Neither Edith's father nor her estranged husband approved of her new lifestyle, and they verbalized their displeasure to her (A+E Television Networks, 2013b). The movie *Grey Gardens* portrays Edith carrying on an affair with her music teacher, Gould; she states in the film that he was the "most brilliant man [she'd] ever met," more so than her father or husband (Sucsy, 2009). Her relationship with him soon ended, leaving Edith alone at Grey Gardens.

According to Beale Jr. (2009), a collection of letters articulates Phelan's financial and emotional support for Edith through 1940, he ran out of money and patience for her lifestyle. He detailed this in his last letter to his family (Beale, 2009, p. 8). The downward spiral continued for Edith in 1942, when she attended her son's wedding late and dressed as an opera singer. Her father was outraged at her behavior and cut her out of his will; he left her a small stipend of $65,000 but turned over control of the money to Edith's sons (A+E Television Networks, 2013b).

On July 29, 1952, Edie was 35 years old and feared for her mother's welfare, since she was alone in the large mansion. Edith asked Edie to move in with her and Edie accepted, claiming that she needed to care for her mother in her declining health. During this time, Edie was at the beginning of an aspiring career in modeling and acting; however, due to her mother's persuasion, Edie left New York City to care for her mother. Edith was only 57 years old at the time and in good health. This began the decline for Edie; she abandoned her lifelong dreams of acting and modeling to live with her mother full time (A+E Television Networks, 2013c). Why the change in heart for Edie with the justification of an ailing mother that allowed Edie to forego her dreams?

Edie wrote a poem that appeared in the book *Edith Bouvier Beale of Grey Gardens: A Life in Pictures*, dedicated to her mother, date unknown, which expressed her feelings about her mother's mental state. The poem paints a picture of a mother whose eyes were sad, despite her laughing lips. Edie described her mother as full of hidden sorrow and wished she had a window to foresee her sadness. As Edie aged in the confines of Grey Gardens, her poetry conveyed her emotional needs and irritation with her mother, the disintegrating living conditions, and the solitude and isolation she felt as a young woman.

The unhealthy dependency between Edith and Edie created lives so closely entwined that they mirrored Grey Gardens at the height of its disrepair, when dead vines covered the entire front of the 28-room mansion. Edith wrote a poem titled "The Sea" that beautifully described the tumultuous sea that pounded within her, paralleling the moans and pleas of the crash of breakers that never ceased, ever torturing her. The surging sea mirrors the never ending wailing and pounding of the wind and sky, leaving her wondering if their cry would sound within her.

Edith and Edie shared one room in the mansion as it began to topple around them. Edith's son asked their mother to sell the home and move to Florida. In the HBO film, she refused, claiming, "It is the only place I feel completely myself" (Sucsy, 2009). There were broken windows and holes in the ceiling, and there was no running water or electricity. Approximately 300 cats and numerous raccoons, rats, and fleas also inhabited the house.

In 1971, Suffolk County deemed Grey Gardens unfit for human or animal habitation and the women were served an eviction notice. Jacqueline Kennedy offered them $32,000 to repair Grey Gardens and allow Edith and Edie to stay in the home (A+E Television Networks, 2013b). However, the mansion quickly fell into disrepair again after the cleanup by the county. Lois Wright (1978) wrote about the floor conditions in her journal in November 1975: "The floor right in front of Big Edie's bedroom upstairs was in terrible condition from all the rain recently. It was dangerous, anyone could have fallen through to the living room" (p. 50). By the time the Maysles brothers began their documentary on the Beales in 1976, the house was in unsanitary condition again, and the brothers had to wear flea collars around their ankles to protect themselves.

In 1976, Edith sustained an injury after falling out of her wheelchair. Her mobility was limited and she struggled to get out of bed. However, she and Edie refused to allow a doctor to come in and assess the injuries, and Edith rarely got out of bed after the fall. She developed infected bedsores. In December, the furnace quit, and according to her daughter, she never recovered from the days of cold. A mirroring of her life, the fierce and radiant fire within her became dormant, just like winter's landscape. In January a doctor was finally called, he encouraged Edith to go to the hospital, but she refused to leave Grey Gardens until the end of her life. She did not want to die in the home because she did not want people intruding on her. She died on February 5, 1977, at the South Hampton Hospital (A+E Television Networks, 2013b).

After her mother's death, Edie left Grey Gardens for New York City. She began a short career as a cabaret singer and dancer. She eventually sold Grey Gardens, but only after the new owners promised to restore the property to its original grandeur. Edie moved to Florida, where she died on January 24, 2002 (A+E Television Networks, 2013c). In a telling request, Edie requested not to be buried next to her mother. She has a grave marker next to her brother Buddy's, inscribed with her quote, "I came from God, I belong to God. In the end—I shall return to God" (Grey Gardens Online, 2009).

Grey Gardens appeared to descend into darkness after the death of Edith's ex-husband Phelan Beale. He left the bulk of his money to his second wife and left a stipend to Edith in the form of a trust handled by her sons, Phelan Jr. and Buddy. In the HBO movie *Grey Gardens*, Edith says she has lived off $150 a month for the last 10 years and that barely paid to keep the lights on and pay for the long-distance bill (Sucsy, 2009). Her sons asked Edith and Edie to consider moving to Florida to reduce the amount of money spent on the upkeep of Grey Gardens. Edith refused to move, claiming she was the sole owner of Grey Gardens and no one could force her to move unless she was removed feet first.

The first pictures taken of the squalor were in 1971. "There are very few, if any, pictures taken during the years in between good times and the 1970s. So for 30 years, the two lived totally reclusive lives, mostly in bed" (Webb, 2009). At the height of the disrepair of the once beautiful, sprawling 28-room mansion, Grey Gardens had a level of "darkness" only seen in black-and-white movies. Gazing at a photo of the once majestic house, I am reminded of a haunted mansion used to film horror pictures. The landscape had become dense with a sea of vines and leaves covering the house and grounds. Edie said in the documentary that she liked the vines that had overtaken the grounds. The doors of the house were bolted at all times and the windows were nailed shut, but breezes wafted through the broken glass and broken frames.

The Beales' next-door neighbor, Gail Sheehy, described the state of affairs on the property in her 2014 memoir *Daring: My Passages*:

> We ducked under ropes of bittersweet hanging from a pair of twisted catalpa trees and tiptoed between humps of cats, too many cats to count, crouched in the tangled grasses, rattling in their throats, mean and wild. Suddenly, we found ourselves at the tippy porch steps of an Arts and Crafts house. Refuse littered the porch. A hand-lettered sign hung from the door: Do Not Trespass, Police on the Place.
>
> (p. 151)

In 1972, the head of the Sanitation Department of Suffolk County was summoned to Grey Gardens due to numerous complaints, "mostly from people downwind," according to the movie (Sucsy, 2009). It was reported that there was no running water or heat and the house was not fit for human or animal habitation per the sanitation department. It was speculated that they were harboring diseased cats. When asked why there was a nonoperable car rusting in the front yard, Edie laughed and stated, "Things start to accumulate after Labor Day." The financial situation of the Beales was dire: the trust had run out, they owed $947 to the heating company, and the grocery store had cut them off as well. There were no working toilets or showers at Grey Gardens and it was home to extensive families of cats and raccoons. The natural order was reclaiming Grey Gardens from the cultural social order. "The wood floors of this once-proud mansion were lumped and crusty with old cat feces; the roof was punctured with raccoon holes" (Sheehy, 2014, p. 153).

Because the women were facing eviction, Edith's niece Jacqueline Kennedy provided a check for $32,000 to complete the cleanup at Grey Gardens. Without this help from Jacqueline, the Beales would have been evicted from the property. Edith did not have the money, nor would she ask for the money to repair the dilapidated mansion. What was the motive behind Jacqueline's generous gift? In the 2009 HBO movie, Jacqueline said she donated the money due to their generosity to her as a child and the fun summers she spent at the property with Auntie Edith and Cousin Edie. Whatever the motive, the mansion was cleaned out, fresh paint was put on the walls over the once beautiful wallpaper, the ceilings were repaired, and new plumbing and heating was installed. At the time of the cleanup, 1,000 bags of garbage were removed from the house.

The once majestic house had a kitchen, dining room, and solarium downstairs and five large bedrooms upstairs. Most of what we know about the poor conditions of Grey Gardens comes from two different sources. One is the documentary film crew, the Maysles, who were granted permission to visit the residence to record and take photographs of the Beales for 6 weeks in 1975. The other is Lois Wright, a painter and palm reader who lived with the Beales for 13 months during 1975. She published a journal of her experiences at the mansion in her book *My Life at Grey Gardens*.

> I had been there before, often, so I knew what to bring. A cot, blankets, food, flashlight, a heavy stick or club, a hat or two, some dishes, what would be needed on most safaris, except a cap gun as I didn't have a real pistol.
>
> (Wright, 1978, p. 2)

The kitchen provided much sunlight during the day but was of little use to the Beales, since they only cooked meals upstairs in their bedroom. Nothing could be left out in the kitchen due to the numerous raccoons searching for food, including soap, which seemed to be a favorite for them. The freezer in the refrigerator did not work, which created a problem storing the Beales' favorite treat, ice cream. Lois wrote that she used the small gas stove to heat water for coffee and expressed concern that the doors were about to fall off their hinges (Wright, 1978, p. 6). Additionally, the floor in the kitchen needed repair; it was sinking near the old coal stove named "Perfection" that had not been in use since the cleaning raid by the county (Wright, 1978, p. 19). Lois hung some of her artwork of colored vegetables in the kitchen to brighten the space. On July 14, 1976, Lois wrote in her journal about the state of the kitchen:

> The kitchen didn't look inviting with the two chairs and table moved against the wall. I noticed another hole in the ceiling near the light fixture. However,

the Silver Cross painting was still over the old coal stove. The small gas stove wasn't being used at all. There was nothing else in the room. It was empty.

(Wright, 1978, p. 153)

Down the hall from the kitchen was a "storage room" that was shrouded in complete darkness. The "icebox room" was named for the temperature in the space. The room was between the kitchen and dining room, and there were large holes in the ceiling where raccoons would jump down to scavenge for food night and day.

There were numerous empty rooms in the mansion that had not seen a visitor in years. The solarium is seen in pictures to have a roof that has collapsed, leaving the room exposed to the elements. The dining room can be seen in photographs to have a ceiling that has broken through the sheetrock, a table with the chairs upside down on top of it, and numerous huge piles of empty cat food cans around the room. In a 1972 photograph, the dining room is seen with a five-foot-high pile of empty cat food tins. The same year, the living room was pictured with parts of tattered sofa, a broken piano, and dusty furniture strewn about, including chairs, a lamp, and a table. The room is also seen with plaster missing from many sections of the ceiling. The living room and dining room show remnants of past memories embedded in the old, dusty, broken furniture of a life once lived but darkened with the turn of unfortunate circumstances for Edith and Edie Beale.

Each one of the five bedrooms upstairs was given a name for reference; the yellow and pink bedrooms, the master bedroom, the boys' bedroom, and the "eye of the house," which was named for its location in the house. The boys' room was seen briefly in the film documentary and is only known to have stored a broken chest of drawers, seashells, and some books. "In a deserted room next to my bedroom, it sounded like a mattress being pushed or slid across the floor" (Wright, 1978, p. 13).

Lois Wright writes extensively about the animals that inhabited Grey Gardens and that moved about at night. Lois lived in the "eye of the house" bedroom for 13 months during her stay at Grey Gardens; this room overlooked the front porch. This was the room where Edie could watch for trespassers and wanderers looking to break in or steal their belongings.

The master bedroom was where Edith slept before the cleanup by the sanitation department in 1972. In the HBO movie, this room is portrayed as having no heat, peeling wallpaper, stained floors, ceiling, and walls, and a large tree branch protruding into the room from a broken window; the queen bed is filthy and stained and there are newspapers strewn around the bed and floor (Sucsy, 2009). Edith vacated the room and moved some of her belongings to the smaller yellow bedroom, presumably because it was more habitable.

After the cleanup there were no beds at Grey Gardens except two twin beds in the yellow bedroom, separated by small side tables where boxes and other food items were kept. The yellow bedroom was where both Edith and Edie lived a majority of the time and where most of the filming of the documentary took place.

According to records, before a photo of Edith was taken in 1971 in her dining room, Edith had not been downstairs for 18 months (Webb, 2009). The yellow bedroom was self-sustaining for the Beales; they cooked their meals on a hot plate that sat on Edith's bed and they had a small refrigerator in the corner of the room. In the HBO film, Edith is shown cooking corn on the cob on this hot plate (Sucsy, 2009). All food that was dropped off on the front porch by the grocery boy was immediately brought to this room, where it was stored until eaten by the Beales or their animals. The large front porch was only used for the purpose of dropping off food or entering and leaving the house; neither of the Beales frequented this area anymore. Edie indicated that it was because the neighbors did not like them; they scared them.

The majority of the room has been shown in the film documentary, HBO movie, and photos as filled with large quantities of trash and newspapers. Other items seen were pots, books, electric cords on the floor, a box of plastic silverware, a ball of string, a tissue box, baskets, cans of cat food, empty bottles, a flashlight, a can of Off insect repellent, a white wooden box on the bed that the telephone sat on, and Edith's gold-framed self-portrait leaning against the dresser on the floor. In one scene from the 2006 movie, Edith is seen eating ice cream in bed, surrounded by numerous trash items; she pulls a paper towel from a roll that she is using for back support to wipe her mouth. As portrayed in 1972 pictures of the yellow bedroom, Edith lay on one side of her twin mattress, and the other side was full of items that seemed to snuggle up to her. The mattress was filthy, and it was shown in the documentary and movie with no sheets, only mismatched blankets and wandering kitties looking to be rubbed. She kept her makeup under her bed and her walking cane hanging on a doorknob next to the bed.

Edith rarely left the yellow room, and if she did, she only ventured to the pink bedroom. The pink bedroom was where the Beales gathered to feel the breeze coming off the ocean, both inside by the open door and outside on the patio; it was shown extensively in the documentary as a gathering place. The patio was not screened in and there were too many flies, fleas, and bees for most to enjoy the space, but Edith believed the sun and air would benefit the cats and she enjoyed the change in scenery. This was where Edie was filmed sunbathing in the 2006 documentary. The space provided a view of the neglected Italian garden below and numerous unmanicured bushes that grew together and formed a jungle of sorts. One could see the Atlantic Ocean off in the distance. "It all seemed like another world . . . even the telephone didn't intrude in this safe, independent, and happy place" (Wright, 1978, p. 14).

Lois's description of Grey Gardens is in stark contrast to the decline of its beauty and capacity, which would suggest an unhappy place. What allowed her and the Beales to feel safe and content amid the decaying nature of Grey Gardens? A home that was unclouded by inconsequential conformities, lives lived in solitude, and a freeing of soul among the backdrop of judgment and scrutiny by outsiders.

Edith Beale always had a love for animals, and her obsession grew after her divorce from Phelan and her short separation from Edie when she went off to New York to pursue her acting career. Bouvier Beale Jr. (2009) wrote that the neighbors called her the "Cat Lady." Albert Maysles (n.d.) wrote that the Beales were confronted with entropic chaos in their lives but accepted this lifestyle without worry:

> They don't worry about holes in the roof but rather feed an invasion of raccoons who chew their way through. They nurture and name countless stray cats who take refuge with them and serve them water in a beautiful old Canton bowl.
>
> (para. 3)

In the original documentary by the Maysles brothers, Edie is seen feeding the raccoons at the end of the hallway from their bedroom. Lois Wright wrote that Edie and Edith used the raccoons as guinea pigs to test any food left by fans on their front porch. Edie believed the food was poisoned, but according to Lois, "All the raccoons led by Buster were very healthy and of normal activity" (Wright, 1978, p. 3). She further noted that the raccoons were always staring down from large gaps in the kitchen ceiling, and occasionally they got carried away with curiosity and would fall from the ceiling. Additionally, both the Beales thought the raccoons should eat at certain times of the day because they believed this cut down on their anger and intent to tear down the house.

Along with the raccoons, the cats were great companions to Edith and Edie. Sheehy (1972), in an article titled "The Secrets of Grey Gardens" in *New York* magazine, recalled Edie saying that old maids didn't need men if they had cats and Big Edie wanting to breed all the cats, 300 cats in total. Sheehy also recalled the Beales fondly referring to their cats as fur people and Edie claiming the 12 cats they had left were not wild. Names of the cats included Little Jimmy, Tedsy Kennedy, Zeppo, Whiskers, Pinky (her babies were Pinky One and Pinky Two), Black Cat, and Champion. Edith says in the HBO movie, "Let's breed cats, Edie. Wouldn't that be fun?" and "I could just elope with these kitties" (Sucsy, 2009). Edith is seen in the documentary and described in Wright's journal as quite charming but demanding when it came to the cats and kittens at Grey Gardens, demanding that Edie feed them numerous times a day and that certain male and female cats be separated and kept from mating. "All the kittens had to be found and brought over to her (Edith). Water had to be heated so their tiny eyes could be wiped with a damp cloth" (Wright, 1978, p. 115). At one time there were 20 kittens needing attention.

Due to the number of cats that inhabited Grey Gardens, fleas were especially rampant throughout the mansion. Lois Wright wrote in July 1975 that every night she had to lay newspapers down on the floor before bedtime to keep the fleas from jumping on top of her while she slept. She recorded that they sounded like Mexican jumping beans hopping up and down.

> In Big Edie's room, the cats and kittens attracted the tiny things, and some cats died because of it. I had no animals in the Eye Room. Nevertheless,

the fleas did get on you in Big Edie's room and sometimes they were still
leaping off me in the post office.

(Wright, 1978, p. 34)

Later the next month, on August 6, 1975, she wrote that the fleas were getting
out of control and just might drive her out of Grey Gardens. "I want to sit outside
but the fleas and flies bothered me. Also there's a strong, unpleasant smell. The
cesspool under the stairs porch has overflowed" (Wright, 1978, pp. 37–38).

In the end, Edith and Edie spent numerous years alone, with just their animals
as companions. Sheehy (2014) sadly recalled Edie's struggle with her mother:
"Mother drove her suitors away, she said. In a final act of negation, she tore out
the faces of her boyfriends from the photographs she saved, so only her image
remained, solitary and sad" (p. 154). She further recalls one summer afternoon where
Edie climbed a catalpa tree and set her hair on fire with a lighter while her cousin
John Davis begged her not to. "And in that act of self-immolation she sealed her
fate as a prisoner of the love of her mother" (Sheehy, 2014, p. 154). They were
still isolated but famous after the airing of the movie *Grey Gardens*, although they
received not even a penny for their story.

Being able to tell the story of the Beales from different viewpoints sheds light
on a new definition of the disorder of hoarding, based on an intimate, personal
relationship with them and not a clinical diagnosis of irrationality, obsessiveness,
or the madness of personal disorganization. The Beales have historically been labeled
as hoarders; however, their story provides a portrait of loss and degeneration into
elemental conditions that contradicts the clinical definition of hoarding, which
centers on the acquisition of objects and an inability to discard. Understanding
their historical backgrounds and their past sorrows and personal tragedies allows
Psyche to have a voice behind the closed-off walls of Grey Gardens. For this reason,
being a witness to the gruesomeness and sadness of two human beings who became
so isolated and mired in waste presents an opportunity to understand their hoarding
condition from a loving perspective, allowing their voices to be heard without
criticism from the Other.

Homer and Langley Collyer: Harlem, New York

For now I note that these two men have also lent their names to Collyer Brothers
Syndrome, a novel psychological disorder that is better known today as hoarding.

(Herring, 2011, p. 159)

When beginning research on Homer and Langley Collyer, the famous brothers
from Harlem, New York, one would expect to find solid evidential background
pertaining to their lives and history. What I found were numerous stories on this
famous duo that have become sensationalized over time by both media and
individual interests. I spent weeks reading and rereading newspaper articles and
books to ascertain the truth about these brothers' background, what was speculation,

and what still remains a mystery. Might this be a preview of what is to come, unearthing the reason why the Collyer brothers hoarded?

Gathering accurate information on the Collyer brothers' lives was difficult. There are only two books written about them, although numerous newspaper articles recounted their histories once their peculiar lifestyle was discovered. The first book is a novel, *Homer and Langley*, written by E. L. Doctorow (2009), who reimaged the life of the Collyer brothers from his point of view using historical documents as a foundation. Distinguishing the factual material from the author's fantasy required reading the book a second and third time after researching the brothers' story through different historical documents. The second book, *Ghosty Men* by Franz Lidz (2003a), is more historically accurate and provides additional background on the brothers' lives and their hoarding setting. The other material for the research is taken from various articles written about them over the years.

Records show the Collyer brothers were born into wealth and privilege as the sons of Herman Livingston Collyer, a prominent Manhattan gynecologist at Bellevue Hospital, and Susie Gage Frost, a former opera singer from a patrician Hudson River Valley family. Herman and Susie were first cousins and told people they could trace their family heritage back to a ship called the *Speedwell* that came to America a week after the *Mayflower*. Langley Collyer was recorded as saying, "Our family is one of the oldest in New York. The first Collyer came from England on the *Speedwell*, which was really better than the *Mayflower*" (Lidz, 2003a, p. 15). In actuality, the Collyers were descended from the Livingston family, which didn't immigrate to America until 1672, 52 years after the *Mayflower* landed in America (Keith York City, 2012, p. 2). Susie came from a seafaring riverboat family whose men seemed to drift around the world in search of beautiful women, and Herman's grandfather, William Collyer, was the largest shipyard owner on the East River. Langley claimed that his parents were born at Tivoli on the Hudson and that his family owned the first steamboats on the Hudson River (Lidz, 2003a, p. 15).

The Collyers had three children: Homer was born in 1881, Langley in 1883, and a daughter, Susan, was born in 1880, but reportedly died at 4 months old. There is no cause of death listed for her. Reports indicate that Dr. Herman Collyer was eccentric himself, paddling a canoe down the East River daily to work at the Bellevue Hospital on Blackwell's Island and then carrying the canoe back home through the streets of Harlem once reaching Manhattan Island (Ask.com, n.d., p. 2). Susie was described as an educated woman who had a great interest in literature, read the classics out loud in Greek to Langley and Homer, and taught them to be gentlemen and scholars (Weiss, 2010, p. 251). During the last half of the nineteenth century, Susie sang operatic roles at the Academy of Music on 14th Street and was known as an unconventional, strong-willed, black-haired beauty with a fine singing voice (Lidz, 2003a, p. 23).

Not much of their background is known prior to the family moving to the Harlem brownstone located on the corner of Fifth Avenue and 128th Street in 1909. Lidz (2003a) wrote that Susie fell in love with Herman, who was an intern at the time, and they moved into a cold-water flat, where both Homer and Langley were born; speculation is that Susie dominated the family (p. 24). "In 1909, the Hamilton family sold the house to Susie G. Collyer. The 1912 city directory lists her in the house with her husband, Herman L. Collyer, and their sons, Homer, born in 1881, a lawyer, and Langley, born in 1883, a musician" (Gray, 2002).

In 1909, when the brothers were in their 20s, the family moved to Harlem, which at that time was a fashionable White suburb of Manhattan (Lidz, 2003a, p. 1). In 1919, Dr. Herman Collyer abandoned his family, moving to 153 West 77th Street. It is unknown why he moved out or whether his wife Susie went with him. George W. Collyer, their nephew, said Susie stayed in Harlem with her boys and chose not to follow her husband because he wanted to turn the Harlem home into a sanitarium and she was tired of the medical field (pp. 24, 55). Lidz also reported that after Dr. Collyer moved out of the brownstone he shared with his family, he visited them daily, or his now 30-something-year-old sons would visit him at his medical office on the Upper West Side: "Langley took his mother downtown to the opera and Homer practiced law on Wall Street" (p. 54).

In 1923, Dr. Collyer died. Susie died 6 years later. There is no recorded information on the nature of their deaths, but in *Homer and Langley*, Doctorow (2009) wrote that it was from the Spanish flu: "The Spanish flu pandemic that hit the city in 1918 . . . swooped down and took off both our parents. My father first because he was associated with the Bellevue Hospital and that's where he came down with it" (p. 16). This is an interesting account of their possible deaths, but there is nothing to legitimize it, and since they died 5 years and 11 years after the recorded flu, this sensationalized report is unlikely.

What is known is that after Herman Collyer's death, all the furniture, medical equipment, and books he had collected over the years were taken back to Fifth Avenue and crammed into the brownstone house his wife and sons shared ("Amazing Stories," n.d.). After Dr. Collyer's death, the purchaser of his property, Mrs. Peter Meyer, brought his own hoarding tendencies into awareness: "Herman's patient found a tremendous amount of 'junk' in the basement when she bought the house after his death, including the Model T Ford, which Langley carted away piece by piece" (Lidz, 2003a, p. 55). After Susie's death, the sons inherited both of their parents' belongings and remained in the 12-room Harlem brownstone, soon becoming reclusive and isolated from the outside world.

By 1925, Harlem had transformed from an upper-middle-class White suburb into the center of African American life in New York. "By themselves for the next 18 years and largely oblivious to the significant demographic change in Harlem, they lived in a self contained world of books, pianos, memorabilia, and Langley's imports" (Weiss, 2010, p. 251). According to Herring (2011), Harlem had an influx of Black migration from 1920–1940, and became a slum replete with "deteriorating houses and immoral bodies" (p. 164). The charm of Old Harlem disappeared with the influx of poor African American families entering the neighborhood. A neighbor who lived near the Collyers described Old Harlem as a wonderful neighborhood where the millionaires of the city used to drive their trotters up and down Lenox Avenue. "There was fine music at Pabst's 125th Street. Ladies went calling in victorias" (Worden, 1953, p. 4). The neighbor told Worden to stick to the main thoroughfares because the district was no longer safe, even in the daytime.

Due to unfounded media reports, the Collyers were thought to have valuables and money stashed within the brownstone mansion; therefore, they were subjected to vandalism. Teenagers would throw rocks through their windows. "Tales of their eccentricities continued to circulate, fueling rumors that the two maintained an extravagant lifestyle behind their closed doors, surrounded by riches and luxuries from Arabia and the Orient" (Keith York City, 2012, p. 3). For this reason, the Collyer brothers boarded up their brownstone windows, covered the ground-floor windows with iron grilles, and bolted their doors. Lidz (2003b) stated that the children in the neighborhood chucked rocks at the Collyers' windows and called them "ghosty men," since they were considered elusive and very rarely seen. In *Ghosty Men*, Lidz (2003a) detailed Langley's sentiment about the neighborhood children: "'These are terrible children,' he said. 'They call me Spook.' They say I drag dead bodies into the house after dark and string them from our old elm tree'" (p. 14). Langley went on to say the children broke his windows, made his life miserable, and even posted a sign on his door saying that his house was a ghost house.

The Collyer brothers' fear and paranoia continued to grow, and they did what they felt would keep them safe: they closed themselves off from everyone. Both Langley and Homer were so isolated from the world that they remained unaware of the Harlem riots that erupted in their neighborhood in August 1943. They had not voted in decades and they heard about the atom bomb on their crystal radio. "The brothers not only ignored the income tax agents, they never registered for the draft in World War II or applied for ration stamps needed for sugar and meat" (Lidz, 2003a, p. 88). As the world carried on without the brothers, they stayed safe within the cocooned walls of their brownstone, living their life the way they felt appropriate. With so many other ways available to express their eccentricities, it is interesting they chose this method of handling their lives.

Homer was the first son, born to Herman and Susie Collyer on November 6, 1881. He was known to be an artist and a lover of music and words (Dirda, 2009). There is no historical information on Homer as a child, but whether fact or fantasy, Doctorow (2009) described a privileged life:

> I [Homer] had tutors for my education and then, of course, I was comfortably enrolled in the West End Conservatory of Music where I had been a student since my sighted years. My skills as a pianist rendered my blindness acceptable in the social world.
>
> (p. 5)

This seems to be contradictory to factual reports that Langley was the musically talented brother.

Doctorow (2009) is the only one who has speculated about the Collyer children's upbringing. He wrote about how Homer and Langley's parents went abroad for one month every year and visited England, Italy, Greece, and Egypt. Their parents shipped home ancient Islamic tiles, rare books, marble water fountains, and busts of Romans. "They were not entirely thoughtless parents for there were always presents for Langley and me, things to really excite a boy, like an antique toy train that was too delicate to play with, or a gold-plated hairbrush" (p. 7). What is interesting is that these items, which Doctorow describes in his novel, were actually found among the hoarded items after the brothers' death.

What is historically known is that Homer was a Phi Beta Kappa at Columbia University, and graduated in 1904 with an MA, LLB, and LLM in Admiralty Law. After his mother died in 1929, Homer took charge of all the financial matters for the brothers. He was reported as having worked on Wall Street. He was described by one of his father's patients as wearing old-fashioned clothes and having a long black beard. She remembers him as being "bright, too bright" (Lidz, 2003a, p. 55). According to Penzel (2011), in 1928, Homer worked for John R. McMullen, a Wall Street lawyer, who later became the family legal advisor when the city stepped in to condemn the brownstone mansion. People who knew Homer at the law firm described him as courteous, cultured, and shy. He dressed in nineteenth-century attire and was said to resemble an 1880s gentleman (p. 2). The attorney John McMullen stated that Homer was quirky and liked people thinking he was a poor eccentric man, and then he would pull out a roll of money and begin a discussion that showed he was not eccentric (Lidz, 2003a, p. 24).

In 1930, Homer worked for City Title Insurance doing research in the New York City Hall of Records. Saul Fromkes, head of the City Title Insurance Company, recalled Homer as being cultured, but by no means a chatterbox about his personal life. However, Homer would occasionally stop by Mr. Fromkes' office on his lunch hour to discuss Greek philosophers (Worden, 1953, p. 15). Mr. Fromkes described Homer as a gentleman, who wore his hair long with thick sideburns, wore a high-collared shirt, and always carried a small roll of newspaper. He was said to have copied his abstracts in a fine, literate hand. Fromkes also reported that Homer walked the eight miles from Harlem every day to work, never springing for the five-cent subway ride, that the soles of his shoes were paper-thin, and that rolled up in his newspaper was his lunch. He offered Homer a retroactive raise and Homer turned around and walked out. He never returned to work or picked up his last check (Lidz, 2003a, pp. 26–27).

After quitting his job, in 1932 Homer bought the building at 2077 Fifth Avenue, across the street from their brownstone, as a business investment for $7,500, pulling the cash from his pants pockets. Homer had intentions of turning the property into an apartment building; however, the property was repossessed in 1943 due to unpaid bills and back income taxes that the Collyer brothers failed to pay over the years (Ask.com, n.d.).

Homer stopped practicing law in 1932, at the age of 51, due to health issues plaguing his eyes and body. According to numerous articles, Homer lost his eyesight in 1933 due to hemorrhages behind his eyes from what is believed to have been a stroke (Keith York City, 2012, p. 3). Bryk (1999) states that Homer was last seen in public in 1932. However, Penzel (2011) reports that Homer's last appearance was January 1, 1940, when Langley and Homer were seen by Sgt. John Collins, a city policeman, carrying a tree limb across the street to their brownstone; Langley guided the branch end and Homer held up the other end (p. 4).

Reports indicate that Homer was crippled by rheumatism in 1940, and for the next 7 years he sat with his legs doubled up to his chin to ease the pain of paralysis and needed around-the-clock care from Langley (Lidz, 2003a, p. 29). "They avoided doctors, treating Homer's illnesses with special diet and rest. Langley said Homer ate 100 oranges a week and treated his eyes by consciously resting them: keeping them closed at all times" (Bryk, 1999, p. 1). Langley felt Homer's blindness could be cured through this special vitamin C diet, black bread and peanut butter, and their father's extensive medical library.

Lidz (2003a) detailed the last incident when Homer was seen alive within the confines of his home. The same officer, Sgt. John Collins, was called to the home after reports that Homer was dead. He followed Langley through the basement and upstairs in mazelike conditions for a half-hour before laying eyes on Homer:

> He was on a cot, a burlap bag beneath him and an old overcoat on the foot of the cot. "I am Homer L. Collyer, the lawyer," the old man said in a deep voice. "I want your name and shield number. I am not dead!"
>
> "Why are you sitting with your knees up to your chin?" the sergeant asked.
>
> "My legs are doubled by rheumatism. I can never lie down again."
>
> (Lidz, 2003a, p. 3)

Homer Collyer was found dead on March 21, 1947, when police from the 122nd Precinct entered the brownstone upon reports from neighbors that there was a dead body in the home. He was found sitting in a chair wearing just a tattered blue and white bathrobe, his shoulder-length grey hair matted and his chin resting on his knees (Ask.com, n.d.). Homer was found after 2 hours of climbing through junk; he was surrounded by boxes and trash. According to the medical examiner, Dr. Thomas Gonzales, Homer was emaciated and dehydrated.

> There was no food in his stomach or his digestive tract, indicating he had nothing to eat or drink for at least three days before he died, which was attributed to his chronic bronchitis, gangrenous decubital ulcer (a large, untreated bedsore), and senile pulmonary emphysema.
>
> (Bryk, 1999, p. 3)

The medical examiner reported he died of neglect. Lidz (2003a) reported that Homer was found with a shriveled apple, rancid milk, and a copy of the *Philadelphia Jewish Morning Journal* from Sunday, February 22, 1920, resting near his right hand (p. 4). His body was dropped to the sidewalk through the window of the brownstone in a khaki body bag. The funeral was on April 1 (April Fool's Day) and he was laid to rest in the family-owned plot at Cypress Hills Cemetery in Queens, New York. "'All we want is for people to let us alone,' said Langley Collyer, the man of polished manners and of questing mind, devoting his years to quiet service to his blind brother. 'A man's home is his castle'" (Lidz, 2003a, p. 92).

Langley was the second son, born to Herman and Susie Collyer on October 3, 1885. Again, Langley's childhood is unknown. There are no historical documents detailing the Collyer children's lives. It is believed that Langley attended Columbia University with his brother Homer, receiving a degree in mechanical engineering and chemistry; however, Columbia denies any record of Langley attending there (Keith York City, 2012). This is ironic considering how little we know about the Collyer brothers and the excess with which they surrounded themselves.

In his novel, Doctorow (2009) wrote that Langley left for the World War in Europe with the AEF and was reported missing. He later resurfaced, having been nursed back to health after being subjected to poisonous gases. "And he had scars. When he removed his uniform I [Homer] felt more scars on his bare back, and also small craters where blisters had been raised by the mustard gas" (Doctorow, 2009, p. 21). There is no historical information that Langley fought in the war. Did Doctorow use the story of Langley going to war to show that he was subjected to trauma, therefore possibly providing a correlation to his hoarding?

Several sources described Langley as having unique attire for the time period. Upon a chance encounter with Langley outside of his brownstone in 1938, Helen Worden (1953) described him as wearing janitor's overalls, a cloth bicycle cap in the style of 50 years earlier, and long grey hair with a Victorian mustache. She stated that he was courteous and cultured. When Langley was last photographed in 1946, he was described as resembling an aging late Romantic poet: he had a long gray mustache with matching long hair and was wearing an old-fashioned bow tie, vest, and formal black jacket with gray striped trousers. This was considered unconventional dress for that era.

Langley gave up his musical aspirations and became a full-time caregiver to his brother after Homer's 1933 stroke, which rendered him blind. Since Homer spent most of the last years blind, Langley had to feed, bathe, and care for his brother around the clock. Langley said that Homer never really slept, he sat with his eyes closed, and he read Shakespeare and Dickens to him from their library. Langley stated that he never slept either, just learned how to relax without sleep so he could be ready to answer Homer whenever he needed something. When Homer first lost his eyesight, Langley would paint the visions that Homer articulated seeing in his blindness, such as beautiful buildings colored red. He said, "Someday when Homer regains his sight, I will show the paintings to him" (Lidz, 2003a, p. 30). He described cooking all Homer's meals and cutting them into tiny pieces so he could eat with a spoon, bathing him, and tending to all his needs. Langley was his brother's keeper.

Because they were sons of a doctor, Langley decided to come up with home remedies to help Homer. Their medical library inside the brownstone consisted of 15,000 books. "Homer and I decided we would not call in any doctor. You see, we knew too much about medicine" (Lidz, 2003a, p. 24). The brothers did not believe in drugs; they believed in physical culture, calisthenics, and massage. Langley was afraid that doctors would remove Homer's optic nerve, creating permanent blindness. He was confident that Homer's vision would return with a combination of diet and rest. After Homer had consumed roughly 67,600 oranges, Langley told the press in 1946 that he believed his brother's eyesight was improving (Lidz, 2003a, p. 24). However, by all reports, Homer was still blind at the time of his death.

Langley's mother Susie is believed to have taught him how to play the piano. Langley never held a job, but he devoted himself to music and was a concert pianist who had performed at Carnegie Hall. Lidz (2003a) mentioned that Langley had memorized 2,500 pieces of music from Chopin to Gershwin, but disliked the classics, even Gershwin; he boasted that he owned 10 grand pianos and had won 10 grand prizes as a concert pianist, and then admitted to not playing in recent years because the pianos were in another room of the house (p. 90).

Langley told Helen Worden that Chopin was his favorite composer and that he owned a piano that was a gift to his mother from Queen Victoria. He also told her that his last concert was at Carnegie Hall, where Ignacy Jan Paderewski, a Polish pianist and composer, played after him. He told Worden that because Paderewski received better notices than he, he decided not to play anymore because there was no use going on, and he now only played for pleasure (Worden, 1953, p. 9). Penzel (2011) stated that whether or not Langley won prizes as a concert pianist, he could not find any historical information to verify his claims (p. 2). When Langley visited Claremont Morris during the acquisition of the house at 2077 Fifth Avenue, they discussed art, literature, and the merits of Chopin and Mozart for approximately 4 hours, and then Langley offered to play a little Chopin before leaving. "Langley complained my piano was badly in need of tuning. Without further ado, he took off his coat and went to work. I must say he did an excellent job" (Worden, 1953, p. 17).

Langley's other love was tinkering with objects that he had acquired throughout the years. Langley created numerous inventions, like a vacuum for the inside of pianos; he hooked up an old crystal set to a storage battery and attempted to use a Model T engine as a generator for their home. In 1938, the Collyers' brownstone was considered gloomy but not messy; however, over the next 5 years, Langley wandered the streets of Harlem at night dragging a carton by a rope and bringing home items that struck his interest. He was seen as far as Brooklyn walking with his carton, collecting items and food along his walk. He was said to have traveled to Williamsburg, 16 miles away, to purchase stale black bread at the lowest cost. Even though the Collyer brothers were not poor, Langley would rummage through garbage cans looking for food. The Harlem brownstone was transformed into a fortress by 1942 due to the large quantities of newspaper, cartons, tin cans, and other refuse Langley collected on a daily basis (Bryk, 1999, p. 2). All the doors and windows of the brownstone were barricaded with books, newspapers, and junk, walling it off and creating a cocoon of safety from the cruel intruders that the Collyer brothers thought inhabited Harlem. Their stuff was both a fortress and insulation from the outside world.

The New York brownstone was already full of items from the brothers' childhood home and Dr. Collyer's home at his time of death, and now it was bursting at the seams with the items Langley brought in from his night excursions. "When Langley brings something into the house that has caught his fancy—a piano, a toaster, a Chinese bronze horse, a set of encyclopedias—that is just the beginning" (Dirda, 2009). Langley's search for the ultimate expression in his objects and his peculiarities in collecting things led him to acquire objects in several different versions. After their deaths, the brownstone where Langley and Homer resided alone for 18 years provided a treasure trove of antiques, books, and musical instruments as well as thousands of newspapers he had collected throughout the decades. Possibly the collected items offered a way for the brothers to stay connected or intimate with history through their introverted means.

When the police discovered Homer's dead body, Langley was nowhere to be found. Rumors began circulating among neighbors that Langley had either abandoned his brother after he died because of grief, or left him to die because he was overwhelmed by the caretaking. Others believed that Langley was also dead inside the home.

Crews began the arduous task of searching the brownstone for Langley, and a manhunt for him began as well. There were sightings of Langley in nine different states, including on a bus heading for Atlantic City and on the New Jersey shoreline (Ask.com, n.d.). Fourteen days into the search, they discovered a man floating in the Bronx River. News reports initially indicated that the man fit the description of Langley Collyer. However, the body was identified as someone else, so the search continued (Penzel, 2011, p. 10).

After a few days of the police searching for Langley at the residence, according to Bryk (1999), a public administrator from New York County took over the case. By the second day, 19 tons of debris had been removed from the home. After 10 days, the public administrator hired six professional moving companies to remove all the articles of value from the home because they were having difficulty moving within the brownstone. Fourteen days into the search for Langley, the moving crew had only reached two rooms on the first floor, and had removed 51 tons of debris. Bryk indicated that the search for Langley continued for 3 weeks inside the home and in the surrounding cities and states. The nineteenth day yielded 103 tons of debris removed from the home as well as the dead body of the missing man (Bryk, 1999, pp. 3–4).

On April 8, Langley's body was found under a pile of newspapers, suitcases, books, tin cans, boxes, and other debris. He was only 10 feet away from where Homer's body had been located 19 days prior ("Amazing Stories," n.d.). Björn Perborg (n.d.) described the gruesome scene when Langley's body was discovered: "His partially decomposed corpse was being set upon by rats and they had eaten half of his face, both hands, both feet and parts of his right thigh." Lidz (2003a) confirmed this fact in his book, saying that it appeared that Langley was turned toward his brother with his arm and gnarled fingers stretched out as if in supplication (p. 132). Speculation circulated that Langley had been dead approximately 2 to 4 weeks.

> Lidz (2003a) described what Langley was wearing the day of his death: He wore four pairs of pants, but no underwear, a herringbone jacket, a red flannel bathrobe, a gray dungaree jacket, and a rat eaten morning coat. Knotted at his neck as an ascot was an onion sack. A burlap bag was fastened to his shoulder.
>
> (p. 133)

This was definitely a peculiar dress for an eccentric man, whether in death or life, and may have sprung the wire on Langley's own booby-trap while he crawled through the debris that filled the room. According to Mcqueeney (2012), "The authorities discovered that Langley had actually been the first to die, killed by one of his many booby-traps he had set up to deter outsiders from coming inside the house of junk" (p. 5). The article reported that Langley died bringing food to his brother Homer when his bathrobe snagged the trap he had set, causing it to collapse on top of him.

It took police over 2 hours to remove the debris from around the body and carry him out of the building. Thomas A. Gonzales, the medical examiner, concluded that Langley died of suffocation, smothered by the debris, and had been dead for at least a month (Penzel, 2011, p. 11).

"The inside is the outside and the outside is the inside. Call it God's inescapable world" (Doctorow, 2009, p. 81). In 1917, the Collyer brothers disconnected their telephone service, citing that they were being billed for long-distance calls they didn't make. Additionally, Langley rationalized to outsiders that they did not need a phone because Homer couldn't lift himself out of bed to answer it and there was no one they wanted to speak to anyway. They had decided to live their lives on their terms. Langley had decided to simplify their lives by not using any utilities, and he simplified their diet as well by eating mostly peanut butter and black bread.

In 1928, their gas and electricity were turned off. "They also seemed to have given up the convenience of running water and steam heat, and began using kerosene to light their home and to cook with" (Penzel, 2011, p. 3). Penzel reported that they obtained water from a public fountain four blocks from their home. The brothers heated the large home with a small kerosene lantern, and Langley attempted to generate his own energy by means of a car engine. Langley and Homer lived much of the time in the dark. Langley indicated that since Homer could not see and had no need for lights and he preferred the house a "trifle shady," there was no need for electricity (Lidz, 2003a, p. 20).

The forlorn brick brownstone on the corner of 128th Street and Fifth Avenue in Harlem is where the Collyers lived from 1909 until their deaths. Helen Worden, a reporter from the *New York World Telegram*, described much of what is known about the brownstone mansion; she covered the Collyer story starting in May 1938. She provided a desolate image of the home in her book *Out of this World*:

> Its storm doors were shut and a portion of the front steps missing. A gaping hole marked the location of what had once been a doorbell. Through splintered glass windows I could see old-fashion wooden shutters drawn tight and evidently latched from the inside. Newspapers littered the areaway. Over the roof arched an enormous elm, like a hangman's tree. Though apparently deserted, the house bore neither a for-rent nor a for-sale sign.
>
> (Worden, 1953, pp. 4–5)

Franz Lidz (2003a) described the outside of the Collyer residence as deserted, with doors bolted, ground-floor windows covered in rusted iron grilles, and the windows all broken, shuttered, or stuffed with paper (p. 3). The windows that remained intact had not been washed in years.

When Police Emergency Squad 6 arrived on the premises to look for the Collyer brothers upon reports that they were dead inside the home, they used axes and crowbars to force entrance, breaking their way through an iron-grille-covered door to the basement in the front of the house. They were unable to gain entry due to the many objects blocking their passage (Penzel, 2011, p. 6). Another report indicates that the NYPD attempted to open the large mahogany front doors, but were not successful, so they removed the doors by the hinges. They were met by stacks of boxes blocking the entrance up to the ceiling (Keith York City, 2012). Penzel (2011) reported that the police then attempted entry through the second- and third-floor windows, but many of the windows had shutters that could not be opened; entrance was finally gained through a window on the second floor, where Homer was found (p. 6).

These descriptions of the Collyers' brownstone bring forth the image of a house kept on lockdown, like a prison. It kept the criminals from entering their sanctuary and provided safety for the brothers from a world they felt was cruel and unstable. The Collyer brothers could have felt like prisoners in their own neighborhood as it changed around them, surrounded by the uncertainty of the time they lived in. Therefore, they created a mirroring of their inward fear to reflect outwardly in their dwelling. Penzel (2011) stated that Langley had fears of being robbed by individuals in the neighborhood and their home became their fortress, complete with trip-wire booby-traps made from debris that could fall on unsuspecting burglars and crush them to death (p. 3). Fear and paranoia created additional isolation for the brothers, keeping people out, but not the rats. The brownstone was turned into a makeshift war zone complete with booby traps and falling debris created by the brothers in rage against the transformation of the neighborhood of Harlem and its insurgents.

A city housing inspector told *The Sun* newspaper that the house was literally rotting. Cracks and holes in the windows and roof allowed the walls and floors to be saturated with water, and the beams of the home were rotted. The house was buckling and crumbling under the weight of the junk, and bricks were falling from the walls (Bryk, 1999, p. 3). The one-time showplace was transformed into a rotting prison and eventual tomb. Nevertheless, Helen Worden could see the glorious past shining through the pervasive decay and dust. When she entered the home, instead of focusing on the piles of junk, she had an amazing eye for the architecture and detail of the Victorian mansion. She summarized her exploration of the Collyer mansion in her book, noting the exquisite facets of the fancy patterned tessellated floor, expensive embossed wallpaper, and a long flight of stairs carved from walnut that matched the enormous woodwork-framed front doors. She noted that the drawing room was covered in a costly light gold and brown figured paper, with a ceiling fresco of wild roses and rose-patterned porcelain medallions. Both the walls and ceiling were dusty and peeling, and the ceiling had fallen in places, revealing wood lathing. The Collyer parlor had the same hand-painted wild rose ceiling and housed wall-to-wall bookcases, a fancy porcelain and brass gas chandelier, a carved walnut mantel that ran the length of the room, and old-fashioned shuttered bay windows from which white-dotted Swiss curtains hung (Worden, 1953, pp. 41–43).

Although there was much beauty in the rooms of the Collyer mansion, every step was taken in caution. "Walking out of the room, I stubbed my toe on the bronze bust of an Indian. Langley's cunningly placed beer-can burglar traps still made exploration risky" (Worden, 1953, p. 42). Langley had carved a network of tunnels through the junk and rigged numerous traps that would not only alert him that someone was in the house, but also crush the intruder to death.

Some people believed that the thousands of cardboard boxes within the home were stuffed with cash (Penzel, 2011, p. 7). These types of reports fueled burglary attempts. "On more than one occasion thieves tried to break in to steal the fortune that was rumored to be kept in the house" ("Amazing Stories," n.d.). Due to the attempted burglaries, Langley's fear intensified, and he continued building and creating traps and tunnels to assuage it. One of his most elaborate traps was created with a large tree limb measuring 20 inches in diameter (Penzel, 2011, p. 9).

In the search for Langley, police removed large quantities of amassed junk. Most was deemed useless and hauled away by the sanitation department. However, among the junk were treasures Langley had managed to collect over the years. Worden (1953) gave a detailed account of her walk through the home when the police were still looking for Langley. Passage into the brownstone began at the basement door. An old stove, numerous umbrellas, several bundles of newspapers, a gas mask canister, and a broken scooter were blocking the entranceway past the basement door (Penzel, 2011, p. 7). Once past this area, one could see rare treasures belonging to the Collyer family housed in the basement. This was where police found the 2,500-volume law library and a large stash of musical instruments, including two pipe organs, a clavichord, a trombone, a cornet, an accordion, and five violins (a 1762 Georgus Rugeri Cremona, a 1784 George Paolo Magini Brescia, and a 1727 Stradivarius cello—all fake). Among the other treasures in the basement were 13 ornate mantel clocks, Langley's sheet music for Chopin's Nocturnes, one metal bust of a girl whose ears and bodice dripped coins, Susie Collyer's unfinished knitting, Dr. Collyer's forms for "Habit Forming Drugs," and a two-headed baby floating in formaldehyde (Lidz, 2003a, p. 129). Worden (1953) wrote that the basement was where they located dozens of boxes containing hundreds of unopened letters, thousands of newspapers, a half-dozen tickets to the 1905 annual excursion of Trinity Sunday School, odd bits of furniture, a box of boys' tops, a nursery refrigerator, and the chassis of the Model T Ford Langley had been tinkering with to create power (p. 36).

Packing cases were blocking the basement stairs to the first floor. Once on the first floor, the police entered the drawing room. "In 3 hours they had gone less than two feet into the drawing room" (Worden, 1953, p. 30). Within the first floor were ceiling-high stacks of boxes, paper, and furniture crawling with rats. Dr. Collyer's 5-foot-wide metal and glass static machine containing numerous balls, cranks, bells, and whistles to treat rheumatism and arthritis was found on the first floor. Dr. Collyer's X-ray machine, a Davis and Kidder's Magneto Electric Machine, his Gladstone with all instruments intact, and a disassembled medical specimen including two human skulls, spine, hands and feet, and a rib cage were found in a wooden canopied crib off the parlor (Lidz, 2003a, p. 130). Keith York City (2012) reports that on the first floor alone, in two rooms, 51 tons of debris were removed along with family oil paintings, toy trains, 14 pianos, chandeliers, tapestries, clocks, 13 Oriental rugs, 5 violins, 2 organs, multiple guns, bowling balls, pickled human organs in jars, and 8 live cats (p. 6). They also found Susie Collyer's hope chest, which contained unused pieces of goods, silks, wool, damask, and brocade, three unwrapped 54-yard bolts of embroidered white curtain material, and unused fine linen towels stamped "Collyer" (Bryk, 1999, p. 3).

The stairs to the second floor were again blocked by packing cases. When the police entered the second-floor bedroom where Homer was found, it was blocked by stacks of newspapers, magazines, rocks, and boxes, and it took them 2 hours to set foot in the room (Worden, 1953, p. 33). As they continued the search for Langley, the police entered a small third-floor skylight room and a portion of the front parlor. Again, they stumbled on newspapers, boxes, grand pianos, portions of a surrey (a horse-drawn, four-wheeled, two-seated pleasure carriage with an open spindle seat), and mountains of trash.

Among the remaining items reported by different news sources were telephone directories, three revolvers, two rifles, a shotgun, ammunition, a bayonet, a saber, a toy airplane, a bugle, a portrait camera, enlarger, lenses and tripods, bicycles and bicycle lamps, a 100-foot rug runner, a 9-foot-tall mahogany clock with a music box inside, Victorian oil lamps and vases, white plaster portrait busts and picture frames, scores of 7-inch gramophone records dating from 1898, sheets of Braille, and a certificate of merit for Langley dating back to 1895 for good conduct (Bryk, 1999, p. 4). Helen Worden found a few more items in her exploration, including an iron printing press, framed photographs, a bone, an egg, a shovel, an old drugstore promo for "Drexel's Belle Cologne," a picture of a pretty smiling girl in a Victorian negligee, a reproduction of a watercolor of St. George and the dragon,

34 saving bank books (11 were canceled, but the total of the other 23 books amounted to $3,007.18), and a walnut-framed mirror 10 feet high with a pink marble shelf (Worden, 1953, pp. 39–42). Penzel (2011) referenced still more items in the Collyer mansion: a child's chair, an automobile radiator, dressmaking dummies, a sawhorse, a rusted bedspring, a checkerboard, a kiddy car, three women's hats, a box of curtain rings, a green toy bus, some lead pipes, a 1914 Metropolitan Opera program, and a beaded lampshade (p. 8).

Living in a hostile Harlem neighborhood and being suspicious of the people who taunted and surrounded them, the Collyer brothers created an internal world of items that brought them joy and peace and a labyrinth to keep them safe. Their need to be self-sufficient and not rely on modern technology allowed the brothers to lead a solitary life—exactly the way they wanted it.

Andy Warhol: famous artist

> A whole day of life is like a whole day of television. TV never goes off the air once it starts for the day, and I don't either. At the end of the day the whole day will be a movie. A movie made for TV.
>
> (Warhol, 1975, p. 5)

Andy Warhol's story seems to fit this statement in his book *The Philosophy of Andy Warhol*. He lived his life with all the glamour and brightness of the art scene and movie industry he was a part of.

There is an abundance of factual information on Andy Warhol; narrowing the information down to the most pertinent facts for the biography was a challenge. Some details of his life may have been left out, but this does not affect the overall research. Andy had a unique doctrine, a philosophy all his own, about how he saw himself, others, and the world.

Andy Warhol came into the world on August 6, 1928, as Andrew Warhola, son of Slovakian immigrants Andrej and Julia, who resided in Pittsburgh, Pennsylvania. Andrej Warhola was a construction worker and Julia was an embroiderer (A+E Television Networks, 2013a). Shortly after Andy's birth, Andrej lost his construction job and the family had to downsize. They moved to a two-room apartment in Pittsburgh's grimy immigrant ghetto, where Andy shared a bed with his older brothers Paul and John. It was a cramped space; the bathtub was in the kitchen, which was convenient because the hot water needed to be boiled on the stove, and the back alley was the communal privy (Greenberg & Jordan, 2004, p. 2). Andy grew up during the Great Depression in the urban surroundings of a smoky industrial city.

According to Greenberg and Jordan (2004) in *Andy Warhol: Prince of Pop*, the Warhola family originated in Carpatho-Ruthenia, a poor farming area of the Carpathian Mountains, and came to America hoping for a better life and more job opportunities. The Warhola family spoke the language Po Nasemu, a mixture of Hungarian and Ukrainian. They settled into the Soho neighborhood among other

Middle Europeans who were seeking the same type of life; however, what they received were dangerous low-paying jobs and cheaply built housing with unsafe sanitation (Greenberg & Jordan, 2004, pp. 3–4). The family maintained their Slovakian culture and heritage while living in the ethnic enclave. Andy recalled his mother reading to him in her thick Czechoslovakian accent. The family was extremely religious; they strictly observed the Sabbath on Sunday and attended the Byzantine Catholic Church, which was a 3-mile walk from their home. Rain or shine, Andy dutifully attended church with his mother during the week and also on Sundays (Greenberg & Jordan, 2004, p. 3).

Andrej was described as having a stern glance that compelled instant obedience from his children. He was a hardworking man who labored 6 days a week, 12-hour days, to keep food on the table and a roof over their heads during the toughest part of the Great Depression. Andrej was frugal with his money and did not drink or gamble like others whose lives were plagued by the same incessant drudgery of the times. People, some of them family, called Andrej a tight-fisted workaholic; Andy later in his life said that he had inherited the capacity for hard work and a thrifty nature (Greenberg & Jordan, 2004, p. 5). "My father was away a lot on business trips to the coal mines, so I never saw him much" (Warhol, 1975, p. 21).

Julia was a stark contrast to Andrej's stern persona: she was kind, loving, artistic, religious, had a good sense of humor, and favored singing and telling mythic stories of the "old country" (Greenberg & Jordan, 2004, p. 5). Julie was an avid supporter of Andy's talent in art, and she bought him his first camera and film projector when he was 8 years old. She would have a profound effect on Andy's life and become a contributor to his art with her old-world penmanship. She moved to New York in 1952 to live with Andy, and continued to mother him into his adult life until her death in 1972 (Aaronson, 2004, p. 265).

Andy's brothers took a paternal role with him due to their father being out of town often for work; they thought he was becoming a sissy, but attempts to toughen him up through sports failed. His brothers enrolled him in the first grade, but Andy only lasted a day and went home crying. Andy was considered shy as a child and often hid behind his mother's skirt when visitors stopped by (Greenberg & Jordan, 2004, p. 6). In the movie *Superstar* by Chuck Workman (1990), Andy's first cousin Christine recalls him as a young boy being "very shy, cute, very different—real different."

Julia coddled Andy; he was the youngest child and for reasons unknown she feared his health was fragile. Her fear came to fruition when 8-year-old Andy contracted rheumatic fever, which in those days could be a death sentence; the only treatment was bed rest. Then the doctor diagnosed Andy with chorea, St. Vitus' Dance, which left him with shaky hands and knees that buckled. He was teased by classmates but revered as special by his teachers and his mother. Andy was prescribed bed rest, where his only activities were reading fashion magazines, coloring and drawing, and watching movies on a projector that his mother had bought him when he was 8 years old (Greenberg & Jordan, 2004, p. 8). Andy's mother showered him with devoted care while he was sick; she encouraged him to color and when he completed a picture, she would reward him with candy. Greenberg and Jordan (2004) stated, "Under the doting gaze of his mother, he lay in bed with his comics and coloring books, drifting and dreaming, free to contemplate and fantasize" (p. 8). Retrospectively, Andy reflected on this: "I think I'm missing some chemicals and that's why I have this tendency to be more of a—mama's boy. A—sissy. No a mama's boy. A 'butterboy'" (Warhol, 1975, p. 111).

At a very young age, Andy's peculiarities began to emerge. He wrote that as a child he was sick a lot, and his sickness was like a little intermission (reference to TV's intermission) where he played with dolls. "I would spend all summer listening to the radio and lying in bed with my Charlie McCarthy doll and my un-cut-out cut-out paper dolls all over the spread and under the pillow" (Warhol, 1975, p. 21). Andy recalls the severe bouts with St. Vitus' Dance as nervous breakdowns, one at 8, 9, and 10 years old, and always at the beginning of summer.

> I never used to cut out my cut-out dolls. Some people who've worked with me might suggest I had someone else cut them out for me, but really the reason I didn't cut them out was that I didn't want to ruin the nice pages they were on.
>
> (Warhol, 1975, p. 117)

His fantasies kept him entertained during his down time as a boy. Andy found escape through popular celebrity magazines and DC comic books, which years later would re-emerge in the form of art imagery as an adult (Andy Warhol Foundation for the Visual Arts, n.d.).

After recovering some from his illness, Andy returned to school, where a teacher recommended he attend the Carnegie Institute on Saturday mornings for a free, gifted children's art class. Many children from Pittsburgh's upper class attended.

> The movies Andy loved showed Hollywood's version of glittering extravagance, but now, on Saturday mornings at the museum, he gained a close-up view of an affluent and privileged way of life that looked out of reach for a Ruthenian boy from a blue-collar family.
>
> (Greenberg & Jordan, 2004, p. 9)

Andy quickly stood out to the art teacher, Joseph Fitzpatrick, and received honor roll several times while attending. Andy lived his life based on the philosophy Fitzpatrick taught his students:

> Art is not just a subject. It's a way of life. It's the only subject you use from the time you open your eyes in the morning until you close them at night. Everything you look at has art or lack of art.
>
> (Greenberg & Jordan, 2004, pp. 10–11)

At a young age, Andy realized art was everywhere he looked.

When he was 13 years old, his father died of peritonitis, brought on by pre-existing jaundice and hepatitis that were contracted while working on a construction site. Andy was traumatized that his dead father was laid out in their small home for 3 days. He hid under his bed crying, refusing to come out. He asked to stay with his aunt until the funeral services were carried out. It is believed that this was where Andy's fear of death began (Greenberg & Jordan, 2004, p. 12). In *The Philosophy of Andy Warhol*, the chapter titled "Death" consists of only one paragraph: "I don't believe in it [death], because you're not around to know that it's happened. I can't say anything about it because I'm not prepared for it" (Warhol, 1975, p. 123). Andy avoided the topic of death. He did not attend his mother's funeral in 1972, and when asked about her well-being by people who did not know she died, he reported that she was fine. As late as 1976, when friends asked about his mother, Andy said, "Oh, she's great. But she doesn't get out of bed much" ("Andy Warhol Biography," n.d.).

When Andy's father died, he left a life insurance policy that allowed Andy to matriculate to college. His father believed Andy had a talent. Another tragedy befell Andy in 1944, his senior year in high school, when his mother was diagnosed with colon cancer. The only option to save her life was a risky surgery to remove portions of her colon. Andy was worried that she was going to die and asked his brothers daily if she had. The brothers took turns caring for Andy during this time and fed him Campbell's soup for his meals. Years later, Andy's art of the soup cans paid homage to the time when his mother was sick and he ate the soup daily.

During his puberty years, Andy was plagued with numerous skin conditions that caused him to be ridiculed by peers and family. He was given the name "Andy the Red-Nosed Warhola" for his blotchy and pale skin that broke out in fiery acne, including a swollen, red, inflamed nose. Due to this relentless teasing, Andy withdrew and became increasingly shy, and his self-esteem and confidence suffered. He would spend his afternoons at the local drugstore, where he sat in a booth and drew people (Greenberg & Jordan, 2004, pp. 13–14). "I had another skin problem too—I lost all my pigment when I was eight years old. Another name people used to call me was 'Spot'" (Warhol, 1975, p. 64). He attributed his skin color pigment disorder to a girl he liked who was two-toned and fascinated him. "Within two months, I was two-toned myself" (Warhol, 1975, p. 64).

In the documentary *Andy Warhol*, directed by Ric Burns (2006), Andy is described as having paralyzing anxiety about his physical appearance and acutely self-conscious. He believed he was totally unattractive, too short, too pudgy, and too grotesque. His greatest source of distress was his thinning hair, which led to his purchase of hundreds of wigs over the years. In his 20s, Andy attempted to have his nose reconstructed and his skin surgically sanded, but these procedures did little to change his appearance. He told his friend Charles that he was from another planet and didn't know how he got here (Burns, 2006). Andy's physical appearance would plague him with insecurities in forging intimate relationships his whole life.

After high school, Andy attended Carnegie Tech, beginning in 1945. He became a leader in his class, even though he was the youngest. While attending Carnegie, he met Phillip Pearlstein, another artist, who planned to move to New York to pursue art studies and asked Andy to accompany him. In 1949, he moved to New York with just his art portfolio from Carnegie, $200 in his pocket, and his mother's advice that if he believed, great, terrific, and crazy things would happen to him (Greenberg & Jordan, 2004, p. 23). "He lived here for almost four decades, establishing a career as a commercial artist, a major modern painter, an innovative filmmaker, a magazine publisher, a socialite, a music promoter, and a totally unique celebrity figure" (Kiedrowski, 2011, p. 6).

Andy loved New York for its potential, and he was starstruck by the city itself. However, he suffered numerous panic attacks and fell into depression while trying to make a name for himself in the art world. According to Greenberg and Jordan (2004), Andy liked the financial security of commercial artwork, but he aspired to be a famous artist. He would spend a considerable amount of time on the phone during night hours and was afraid to fall asleep because he thought his heart would stop, so he would talk to anybody who answered his calls and begged them for their ideas (Greenberg & Jordan, 2004, p. 45). However, Andy struggled with close relationships, not only because of his skin condition but also because of a fear of being hurt. "When I got my first TV set, I stopped caring so much about having close relationships with other people. I'd been hurt a lot to the degree you can only be hurt if you care a lot" (Warhol, 1975, p. 26). Andy became the "nobody" in the room, saying that people came to his Factory gatherings not to see him, but because the door was open. "They weren't coming to see me, they came to see each other. They came to see who came" (Hackett & Warhol, 1988, p. 151).

Working for *Glamour* magazine in 1950 made Andy a successful commercial artist, known for his unique whimsical style and blotted line and rubber stamp technique (A+E Television Networks, 2013a). He began to shift from commercial art to painting toward the end of the 1950s. By the 1960s, Andy was producing numerous groundbreaking works including the Campbell's Soup cans, portraits of famous movie stars like Marilyn Monroe and Elvis Presley, and the Coke bottle series. Additionally, his work from this time period was a lively expression of his sexual and artistic arousal. "He made thousands of beautifully rendered sketch-book portraits of young men and erotic drawings of male couples" (Aaronson, 2004, p. 246). He may have asked people for their ideas, but Andy followed his own instincts and chose people and subjects that captured and held the public's attention. "New Yorkers couldn't decide whether Andy was serious or perpetrating a gigantic joke at their expense, but they flocked to see his startling work" (Greenberg & Jordan, 2004, p. 54). By 1962, ten years after moving to New York, Andy had achieved fame as an artist.

In 1964, Andy opened up his own art studio called The Factory, a 3,000-square-foot building where he worked on large-scale paintings. It soon became a premier cultural hotspot for wealthy socialites and celebrities to gather and party (A+E Television Networks, 2013a). By 1970, Andy had written several books and produced more than 60 films. In 1980, he moved into television, hosting two of his own shows. Andy was widely criticized for his movies' subject matter and titles, including *Sleep* (1963), for which he filmed a man sleeping for 6 hours, and *Eat* (1963), a man eating a mushroom for 45 minutes.

A troubled writer named Valerie Solanas who thought Andy was trying to steal one of her manuscripts shot him at The Factory on June 3, 1968. A single bullet pierced seven of his major arteries, and he was declared dead upon arrival at the hospital. However, his life was saved after 5 hours in surgery (Aaronson, 2004, p. 139). Andy had a long road to recovery, and this event forever changed the way he perceived his health and his own mortality. "The attempt on his life left him permanently and severely affected, and he was forced to wear a surgical corset" (p. 110). Aaronson also reported that Andy wore a crystal around his neck to foster health and emotional well-being for a period of time in the 1980s (p. 110). Andy said, "The fear of getting shot again made me think I'd never again enjoy talking to someone whose eyes look weird. But when I thought about that I got confused because it included almost everybody I really enjoyed" (Greenberg & Jordan, 2004, p. 114).

Andy feared being alone at The Factory after this incident, and he also refused to testify at Solanas's trial even though she continued to terrorize him from jail with threatening phone calls. She was deemed mentally ill and sentenced to 3 years in prison. People who knew Andy after the shooting said he sort of died after he was shot: his energy level went down and it appeared he couldn't handle crazy people anymore. They reported he wanted a simpler life (Workman, 1990).

Andy's way of thinking and seeing the world was unique. He had a way of living his life that was distinctive to his surroundings, eccentric and opulent. According to A+E Television Networks (2013a), Andy's personal life was the subject of much debate and consideration. What is known about Andy is that he was a gay man and much of his artwork contained homoerotic imagery and motifs, which were shunned by the art world at the time. Andy had a nickname that was given to him by his employees at The Factory: "'Drella,' a contraction of Dracula and Cinderella, the first alluding to his cold-blooded demeanor and the second to his homosexuality" (Aaronson, 2004, p. 301).

Andy clearly relished his celebrity status. However, the dynamics of his thinking and inner life have proven elusive. "Warhol's life and work simultaneously satirized and celebrated materiality and celebrity" (A+E Television Networks, 2013a). When he was asked why he painted the famous Campbell's Soup cans, his response was "I wanted to paint nothing. I was looking for something that was the essence of nothing, and that was it" (Andy Warhol Foundation for the Visual Arts, n.d.). Andy believed people just wanted to be stars, and he coined the phrases "15 minutes of fame" and "superstar" (Workman, 1990).

Andy had a weekly "rut" he kept to and didn't deviate from unless forced to. He had a daily routine he called "gluing" that included washing his face, adjusting his silver hair, and maybe changing his clothes if it was going to be a busy evening out on the town. He frequented the same grocery store daily for 12 years. "I lived next to Gristedes grocery for twelve years, and every day I would go in and drift around the aisles, picking out what I wanted—that's a ritual I really enjoyed" (Warhol, 1975, p. 79). He also kept a daily diary from November 24, 1976, through February 17, 1987. He would call Pat Hackett, his part-time typist, and dictate the previous day and evening's events down to where he went and how much he spent. Pat was expected to transcribe this into a living documentation of Andy's life—his own personal narrative (Hackett, 1989, pp. xvii–xviii).

> Nothing was too insignificant for him [Andy] to tell the Diary. These sessions—what he referred to as my "five-minutes-a-day job"—would actually take anywhere from one to two hours. Every other week or so, I'd go over to the office with the typed pages of each day's entry and I'd staple to the back of every page all the loose cab and restaurant receipts he'd left for me in the interim—receipts that corresponded to the amounts he'd already told me over the phone. The pages were then stored in letter boxes from the stationery store.
>
> (Hackett, 1989, p. xix)

While in New York, Andy frequented a club called Serendipity 3, the first coffee house boutique. According to the Serendipity 3 website (n.d.), "Andy Warhol declared it his favorite sweet shop, and paid his chits in drawings." In the movie *Superstar*, the owner, Steven Bruce, had a unique assessment of Warhol: he said that Andy had an artistic eye for beauty. He was anemic, evident in his pallid skin and hair, and he probably didn't have the strength for sex. Steven went on to say he thought sex was mostly visual for Andy; his idea of sex was by having beautiful people around him (Burns, 2006). Andy wrote, "I never met a person I couldn't call a beauty" (Warhol, 1975, p. 61). He was also quoted in his book as saying, "Sex is more exciting on the screen and between the pages than between the sheets anyways" (p. 44) and "But I'd rather laugh in bed than do it" (p. 49).

Gerard Malanga, a handsome 21-year-old aspiring poet and artist who worked for Andy, said that Andy had a knack for making people feel important and increasing their self-esteem. "It's as if he were collecting people. He has a hypnotic power to create a personality for someone . . . the secret to Andy's success was his own self-effacement" (Greenberg & Jordan, 2004, p. 60).

Andy Warhol died on February 22, 1987, at the age of 58, from complications stemming from gallbladder surgery. His fear of death, including hospitals and operations, could have influenced his waiting, even though in pain, to have the operation. Andy omitted from his daily diary to Pat Hackett that he went to the doctor on February 14 for a collagen treatment and complained of gallbladder pain, but the pain subsided on Sunday and he went back to work. On Friday, February 20, Andy was admitted to the hospital as an emergency patient. On Saturday his gallbladder was removed and he appeared to recover from surgery; he watched TV and made phone calls to friends. However, for unknown reasons, he died the following morning (Hackett, 1989, pp. 806–807).

What shocked the public about Andy were both his cutting-edge artistry and his cutting-edge celebrity status and unique lifestyle. During the mid-60s, the drug culture, gay liberation, and sexual revolution were at their peak, and at the crest of it was Andy, shouting terms like "I don't believe in love" and "I want to be a machine" (Greenberg & Jordan, 2004, p. 64). Andy Warhol wrote an entire book, *The Philosophies of Andy Warhol*, describing his unique philosophies on subjects including love (puberty, prime, senility), beauty, fame, work, time, death, economics, atmosphere, success, art, titles, The Tingle, and Underwear Power. Below are a few excerpts from this as examples of his distinctive and abstract style of thinking:

> The thing is to think of nothing, B. Look, nothing is exciting, nothing is sexy, nothing is not embarrassing. The only time I ever want to be something is outside a party so I can get in.
>
> (Warhol, 1975, p. 9)

> If I ever have to cast an acting role, I want the wrong person for the part. I can never visualize the right person in a part. The right person for the right part would be too much. The wrong people always look so right to me.
>
> (Warhol, 1975, p. 83)

> I suppose I have a really loose interpretation of "work", because I think that just being alive is so much work at something you don't always want to do. Being born is like being kidnapped. And then sold into slavery. People are working every minute. The machinery is always going. Even when you sleep.
>
> (Warhol, 1975, p. 96)

> After being alive, the next hardest work is having sex.
>
> (Warhol, 1975, p. 97)

> Your mind makes spaces into spaces. It's a lot of hard work. A lot of hard spaces. As you get older you get more spaces, and more compartments. And more things to put in the compartments.
>
> (Warhol, 1975, p. 143)

> Every minute is like the first minute in my life. I try to remember but I can't. That is why I got married—to my tape recorder. That is why I seek out people with minds like tape recorders to be with. My mind is like a tape recorder with one button—Erase.
>
> (Warhol, 1975, p. 199)

> My favorite simultaneous action is talking while eating. I think it's a sign of class.
>
> (Warhol, 1975, p. 199)

> My favorite thing to buy is underwear. I think buying underwear is the most personal thing you can do, and if you could watch a person buying underwear you would really get to know them. I mean, I would rather watch somebody buy their underwear than read a book they wrote.
>
> (Warhol, 1975, p. 229)

Andy's style of speaking and presenting himself to the public and media kept people wondering who he was and what was the meaning behind his artwork. His eccentric style and life attracted an entourage of beautiful and outrageous people who catapulted him into fame through his art and movies. He led an elusive and obtuse existence to many people who attempted to follow him, creating immense curiosity about his life and art.

Andy wrote, "At the end of time, when I die, I don't want to leave any leftovers. And I don't want to be a leftover" (Warhol, 1975, p. 112). However, contrary to this statement, he left behind 570 cardboard boxes, 40 filing cabinets, and one large trunk filled with mementos. He had a love for shopping, and went daily. He kept everything that came into his possession; his life became art. He was an obsessive collector and would set out on buying sprees at auction houses and antique stores; he particularly liked flea markets, where he would purchase objects to add to his collection (Aaronson, 2004, p. 18). Alastair Sooke stated in his 2007 article about Andy that he was a shopaholic and inveterate collector who threw nothing out. His studio was jam-packed with all the bric-a-brac he had collected since moving to New York in 1949.

Given his trouble throwing anything away at his four-story Manhattan townhouse, Warhol amassed a considerable hoard. Only the bathroom and kitchen of the house looked normal. The townhouse was jammed with shopping bags filled with antiques, clothes, books, and other artifacts from his daily expeditions, boxes, piles of furniture, and even a drawer of gems worth $1 million (Plushnick-Masti, 2009). Andy moved several times over the years when he needed additional space to house his shopping and collecting habits. In 1960, he quickly filled up his brownstone with antiques, artwork, and electric junk from every corner of Manhattan. Filling his townhouse with furniture and antiques made it increasingly difficult for him to work on paintings. In 1964, he decided to purchase The Silver Factory—3,000 square feet to house his collection of objects and his large silkscreen canvases and artwork (Kiedrowski, 2011, pp. 12, 15).

In 1973, an employee of Andy's suggested he carry a box around to drop his items into to create some sort of order. "Warhol discovered that he loved filing away the detritus of his life, so much so that he began to hoard his possessions in boxes until his death" (Sooke, 2007). Warhol kept a box next to his desk and all items, worthless or valuable, went into it. When the box was full, Andy taped it closed and wrote the month and date on it. Pat Hackett had a firsthand viewing of the boxes Andy filled to capacity. Working with Andy daily, he saw the 10" × 18" × 14" brown cardboard boxes fill up with letters, invitations, magazines, and gifts from fans. Once one was filled, a new identical empty box would take its place (Hackett, 1989, p. xvii).

These time capsules, as Andy called them, rank as the most extensive collection of incidentals of any artist. They are an assortment of windows into who he was, what he was doing, where he was going, and the people he knew (Hannon, 2008). "Another way to think of the Warhol time capsules would be as a giant, three-dimensional diary" (Pilkington, 2007). Andy saw his time capsules as conceptual artwork, a self-portrait that captured the spirit of his age. Several times, he considered exhibiting them, and he even planned to sell his box collection. "His idea was each box should be sold, unseen, for the same price, purchasing them would be a game of chance, in which there would be winners and losers, depending on which items you ended up with" (Wrbican, 2007). On average there were about 200–400 items in each box (some contained as many as 1,200 items); some contained valuable memorabilia and others contained worthless trash.

After his death, Andy's boxes became famous and drew enormous attention from onlookers wanting to see the contents. The collection of boxes is currently kept in air-controlled rooms, lined up neatly like urns, in the Warhol Museum in Pittsburgh.

According to Pilkington (2007), only 91 of the 611 capsules have been opened, and only 19 have been analyzed and recorded. A grant of more than $600,000 from the Andy Warhol Foundation has paid for three archivists to sift through the contents of all the capsules, recording, catalogue, and properly preserving the items. The project is expected to take between 3 and 6 years.

> The end goal is providing not only a detailed physical description of each item but information about where it came from, what its purpose was, and, hopefully, its role in Warhol's life so that, eventually, it can be electronically tracked in a web-based database.
>
> (Hannon, 2008)

A media frenzy began when word spread of the sealed boxes left behind by the famous artist. In 2009, archivists began blogging about the "Object of the Week" (Plushnick-Masti, 2009), and there are videos online of the time capsules being opened for the watchful eyes of fans. Additionally, there have been three ticketed events to watch the opening of a box. Audience members attended out of curiosity about the items in the boxes; even the catalogers didn't know what was inside, which made it all more exciting. Audience member Chris Rauhoff stated, "I envision the time capsules a little bit like Mary Poppins' satchel, they're going to reach in there and pull out a tall lamp or a puppy dog" (Keene, 2013).

Matt Wrbican (2007), the chief archivist who has been sorting through the boxes for the last 16 years, states that it is easy to label the items as junk, but they are archives increasing in value as the years pass. What types of items caught the media's attention? Lauren Ober (2013) explored the contents of one box that included a small tin holding dead bees, nail clippings that belonged to a fan, and little paper circles that came from a hole punch. The museum has indexed more than 3,000 items, from a valuable Tyvek suit covered in Jean-Michel Basquiat's scribblings to a less valuable tube of Preparation H. Erin Byrne, another archivist on the project, stated, "We work more with the intimate side of Warhol. His prescriptions, his shampoos, his acne medication, his letters from family. These are things that blow people away" (Ober, 2013).

There were a lot of outlandish items found, including a pizza, pizza dough (infested with weevils), a slice of Caroline Kennedy's birthday cake, coffee sachets, dried Palm Sunday leaves, bundles of ribbons, candy wrappers, a plastic rosary that glowed in the dark, taxi cab receipts, fan mail, a knit shawl belonging to his mother, numerous financial documents, insurance policies, invoices, un-cashed checks to his mother, movie tickets, a gold Tiffany's dog tag inscribed "Archie" (Warhol's dachshund), and political leaflets. In other boxes he hoarded biscuit jars, native American folk art, taxidermy specimens (including a Great Dane dog and an African lion), half-used bottles of perfume, autographed photographs of movie stars, World's Fair souvenirs, cowboy boots, dental molds, and his trademark white wigs (Pilkington, 2007). Additional outlandish items have been catalogued by Matt Wrbican (2007), who discovered a set of porcelain cutlery and menus from Andy's trip on the Air France Concorde, restaurant bills, newspaper clippings, unpaid invoices, pornographic pulp novels, airline tickets, supermarket flyers, postage stamps, and Chubby Checker LPs.

From TC 350, items discovered were an envelope with used stamps, a German magazine marking the twentieth anniversary of JFK's assassination, a sampler for Maxwell House coffee, a poster for the opening night of Club Limelight, a flyer for a party at Studio 54, a biography of James Dean by David Dalton, and a Lionel Richie album still in cellophane. In TC 64, from the years 1961–1971, among the items recovered were an $8,935.29 invoice from MGM Records for the year's earnings of the Velvet Underground and a get-well card from Edie Sedgwick sent after Warhol was shot. Several boxes contained gay magazines (Pilkington, 2007).

Some of the favorite items catalogued by chief archivist Wrbican included a 2,000-year-old mummified foot belonging to an ancient Egyptian (Andy Warhol had a foot fetish), a Ramones 45 record signed by Joey Ramone, a piece of orange nut bread (with a signed note from his cousin telling him to enjoy it with coffee), and a naked photograph of Jackie O signed "For Andy, with enduring affection, Jackie Montauk" (Plushnick-Masti, 2009). Wrbican (2007) also found Andy's invitations to the White House and the "party of the century," Truman Capote's Black and White Ball; his ticket to Maria Callas's debut at the Metropolitan Opera; and his pass to the scandalous New York disco club Xenon.

There were some valuable art items found among Warhol's collection that caught the interest of art dealers. Discovered were 1,659 pieces of Russell Wright pottery, 72 Navajo blankets and rugs, 61 lots of early nineteenth-century American furniture, 37 art deco cigarette cases, 33 works by Man Ray, 18 by Marcel Duchamp, and 12 by Rauschenberg (Muchnic, 1988). Other rare finds were a set of cards from Yves Saint Laurent raving over a portrait Warhol painted of him, a rare diary with 5–6 entries from Andy while in Paris, a pair of Clark Gable's shoes, never before seen pieces of Warhol's early art (including a watercolor painting of a series of flowers), and a handful of drawings from 1950 along with work from his time as a student at Carnegie. Let's not forget the few odd items in the same box as the valuables: Chloraseptic spray, a still-inflated Batman toy, a porcelain doll, and a tin of meringues (Hannon, 2008).

As many as 200,000 items were found either in boxes or in his home. One wonders why Andy held onto so many items over his lifetime. It seemed his art was indicative of his collecting of objects. Over his life, Andy created over 10,000 paintings, drawings, and sculptures, which is considered to be an astronomical amount in the art world. His intensity for painting and creating rivaled his intensity for shopping and collecting. He was an intense man with an incredible passion for the things he loved.

Ida Mayfield Wood: New York socialite

One's value and worth is in the eye of the beholder—or at least this was the case for Ida Mayfield Wood. She lived a life of secrecy and wealth and created an illusion of how she wanted people to see her. "Her secret remained unexposed during her lifetime. The drama of her death as a recluse, the discovery of her concealed fortune, and the search for her true identity made headline news in the 1930s" (Cox, 1964, Preface). The process of discovering Ida's identity spanned 3 years after her death, when an investigation was necessary to discover the rightful heirs to her fortune. One man alone discovered the truth: Joseph Cox, counsel for the Public Administrator of New York County.

Ida Mayfield Wood was born to parents Tom and Ann Crawford Walsh, and her birth name was Ellen Walsh. According to Cox (1964) in *The Recluse of Herald Square*, her parents originated from Ireland. Tom worked in the textile industry there, where he met Ann, and they married on February 7, 1836. They eventually emigrated from Ireland to England, and finally settled the family in Massachusetts. Ellen was born in England and raised in Massachusetts; eventually she moved to New York in 1857 (Wood, 2010, p. 3).

Cox (1964) was able to trace Ellen's family tree and listed her maternal grandparents as Patrick and Anne Crawford of Dublin, Ireland. He verified that Patrick owned a bakery in Dublin and that the business had been passed down within the family through the generations. Cox also affirmed that Ellen's parents had 11 children throughout their marriage; six of the children died in infancy (John, Elizabeth, Eliza, Thomas, Thomas Francis, and an unnamed child), one (Louis) drowned at age 13, and four children lived into adulthood (Ellen, Mary Ann, Michael, and Emma).

Cox (1964) put together the truth of Ida's life through numerous documents found in her apartment after her death. He located an 1846 burial receipt that was found in Ida's possessions, another receipt for her father's burial in San Francisco in 1864, and a letter dated 1866 indicating that Ida had forwarded money for the care of her brother Michael to the House of the Guardian Angel in Jamaica Plains, Massachusetts ("Hibernian Chronicle," 2011). Cox found a rose-colored book that contained cryptic writings in Ida's own hand about the details of the death of her mother and location of her grave in New York. The notebook also contained information on the death of her father in California and an entry regarding her brother's death from drowning. "It was, said Cox later, 'the Rosetta Stone of the Ida E. Wood mystery'" ("Hibernian Chronicle," 2011). With all these documents in his possession, Cox was able to locate the burial site of all of Ida's deceased immediate family members at the Catholic Cemetery in Cambridge, Massachusetts. Ann Walsh had erected a headstone in loving memory of her husband Thomas, his mother Margaret, son Thomas, an infant son, and son Louis (Cox, 1964, p. 134). Cox testified to this information in court, providing proof of Ida E. Mayfield's true identity as Ellen Walsh. Cox was perplexed about why she would go to great lengths to hide their true identity, deceiving so many people, even up to her last breath on earth. Through his investigation he was able to put together a timeline of events, uncovering her possible intentions and motives.

All of Ida's family members were recreated to fit her drama, a story she told to anyone who would listen. This was where the story of Ida's life in New York became confusing; contradictions in her stories and dates quickly followed.

> It was after Louis's death in 1865 that finally ended the Walsh era in Malden. Less than a month after he was drowned, Ida's sister Mary sold the house, and with her brother Michael, her sister Emma, and her mother, came to New York to live, and there the Walshes were transformed, in a manner and for reasons we did not yet understand, into Mayfields.
>
> (Cox, 1964, p. 142)

According to Ida, she and her husband Benjamin Wood were married in a private ceremony in 1857 and repeated their vows in 1867; however, no record of the 1857 marriage exists. It is believed that Ida created this story to conceal the identity of her sister Emma from the public and pass her off as the legitimate daughter of her and her husband. Marriage records from the Catholic Church were located indicating that Ida married Ben in 1867 under the name Ida Ellen Walsh Mayfield; a dispensation from the Catholic priest was found referring to her as Ida Ellen Walsh ("Hibernian Chronicle," 2011).

Additionally, before Ida met Ben, his first wife Catherine had died in 1850. In 1860, the census had him living with the two children he had with Catherine, as well as a woman named Delia Wood and her parents. Then on August 19, 1867, a death notice appeared for Delia, and shortly thereafter Ben and Ida were married. This raises the question: who was Delia and were Ben and Delia ever married? No proof of this marriage has been found, but the 1860 census did not have Ida and Ben living together as husband and wife (Cox, 1964, p. 75). Cox discovered that in 1859 Ida was using the last name Harvey, and after her death they found silver with the letter "H" engraved on it that was purchased by Ben. Also, in 1864 she purchased a home using the name Ida Harvey, and Ben witnessed her signature (Cox, 1964, pp. 76–77).

Cox continued to dig further and revealed still more inconsistent and puzzling information. When the 1870 census was taken, ages and names were given incorrectly or left out altogether. Ben was listed as 45, but he was 50 at the time; Ida was listed as 40, but she was 32; and the children were listed as Emma, Henry, and Benjamin. Henry was listed as 10 years old, but he really was 21; the older child by the name of Henry was completely left out of the census; Emma and Henry's birthplace was listed as Kentucky, Ida's as New York; and Benjamin's as Louisiana. However, 10 years later, the 1880 census had the birthplaces for Ida and Henry listed as New Orleans and Emma's as New York. Benjamin was not listed on the census this time because he was married and living with his wife at his own residence (Cox, 1964, pp. 92–93).

Sometime after her marriage to Ben, Ida recreated her past with a new cast of characters to suit the new lifestyle that she had fashioned for herself in the high society of New York:

> By 1872, Ida's mother Ann Walsh, widow of Thomas, a hawker or itinerant trader, had become Mary E. Mayfield, widow of Henry, New Orleans sugar planter; her daughter Mary had become Mary E. Mayfield, and her son Michael had become Henry Mayfield.
>
> (Cox, 1964, p. 142)

In a letter dated October 17, 1887, found among Ida's possessions and given to her by Father Young, who officiated at their wedding, Ben divulged to Father Young in confidence that Emma, who was perceived to be his adopted daughter, was really Ida's sister. He went on to say that he wanted to provide for her monetarily in case of his death and that Emma did not know the truth about her relationship to Ida. He named Emma in his will as his daughter and hoped never to have to divulge this information about her true identity (Cox, 1964, pp. 94–95). Cox stated that as far as he knew, Emma died not knowing her true identity.

Cox wrote the following about his sense of the conspiracy: "The documentary evidence I had offered raised a clear inference, I believed, that Ida, her sister Mary, and her mother were actively engaged in efforts to conceal their origins and identity" (Cox, 1964, p. 190). The surrogate was quoted in *The Hartford Courant* as saying, "[Ida] was plainly actuated by her desire to suppress her humble origin and to assume an alleged social standing in the period before and after her marriage to Benjamin Wood" ("Ida Wood's Early Life," 1937, p. 8). Cox's theory was that during her childhood in Ireland, Ida witnessed extreme poverty, slum conditions, and the Black Plague that swept through the county: "From her earliest memories, Ellen Walsh knew insecurity, hardship, anxiety, and poverty. No doubt she understood something about hunger too, and the fear of powerful forces outside her ken which she did not comprehend" (Cox, 1964, p. 228).

Growing up in such conditions can produce a lasting effect on how one chooses to live one's life into adulthood. Ellen decided that in order to have a new beginning out of the poverty she knew, she needed to assume a new identity and become assertive and creative with the background story of her new life. The persona of Ida was born when she was 19 and forever changed the course of her life. Once she achieved her coveted niche in the high society of New York, she was determined to retain her position as an equal, no matter what further deceptions she might need to engage in.

Nothing is known about Ellen's life before she came to New York. Once in the city, Ellen recreated herself and changed her name to Ida E. Mayfield. "What Ida did for a living, where she lived, who her friends were or whether she had any friends at all, no one can be certain" (Cox, 1964, p. 71). What is certain is that Ida arrived in New York in 1857 at the age of 19. Because she was from a poor, working family, there was purpose in Ida coming to New York. She did not come looking for work, but rather to make a name for herself: to be rich, respected, and admired by high society. Ida was a nobody, but she was beautiful and had studied how to be a lady. "Ida's sensible, direct mind told her there was only one way to achieve such eminence, and that was to marry into it. She cast about for a rich man" (Cox, 1964, p. 72).

The man she sought after was Benjamin Wood, a 37-year-old married businessman and politician. Benjamin's brother was Fernando Wood, mayor of New York at the time, which allowed Ben access into the gilded society of the city. In the ordinary course of events, Ida would never have crossed paths with Benjamin Wood, who owned the *New York Daily News*. "The evidence strongly suggests that Ida, a girl of extraordinary resourcefulness, took a direct route to Ben's heart, after hearing and reading of his exploits as a young man-about-town" (Cox, 1964, p. 73). After Ida's death, a letter dated May 28, 1957, was found in her suite that alluded to how they met. The letter was a direct request to meet him and be interviewed by him for agreeable intimacy, describing herself as "not extremely bad looking" and "knowing a little more"; Ben did meet with Ida and was pleasantly surprised (Abbott, 2013). Abbott detailed the beginning of the lies Ida began to spin: "She told him she was the daughter of Henry Mayfield, a Louisiana sugar planter, and Ann Mary Crawford, a descendant of the Earls of Crawford." She portrayed a true southern belle, a rich and innocent girl.

They were inseparable after the first meeting and she immediately became his mistress. "Ben gave Ida what she wanted from the beginning—money, jewels, and social position—but he also gave her what she hadn't bargained for: love" (Cox, 1964, p. 97). During their whirlwind first years as a married couple, Ida rode the coattails of an elusive high society. In 1860, the Prince of Wales visited the city and a ball was held for him that became the most exclusive event New York had ever seen. People clamored to get invitations to the ball and have a chance to dance with the prince. He danced with many of the single and married ladies at the ball, including Ida. "He must have been impressed by Ida's beauty, which added further glamour to an occasion already so breathtaking that guests could never forget it" (Cox, 1964, p. 81). Ida never forgot this moment in her life.

When she met President Lincoln less than a year later, it made a different impression on Ida because her husband Ben and brother Fernando did not favor

Lincoln and his ideas. They addressed President Lincoln as just "Mr. Lincoln" (Cox, 1964, p. 83). "For a while the couple lived the high life: elegant dinner parties and fancy balls and lengthy trips to Europe, with Ida always draped in the most fashionable clothes and wearing the most expensive jewelry" (Wood, 2010, p. 2). Her fairy-tale life was not without turmoil, but she learned how to manipulate situations that would benefit her. Whether it was attracting Ben by sending him a letter highlighting her beauty and intelligence over his current wife's or having Ben provide monetary compensation for his bad behaviors, Ida knew how to control situations in her life.

Ben was also known as a gambler. Cox (1964) detailed what a talented and careless spender he was; he gambled large sums of money, winning $100,000 and $150,000 hands, and he even wagered the *Daily News* in one card game. Thankfully for him, he won that time. However, he also lost considerable monies gambling. He would gamble for long periods of time at John Morrissey's gambling hall on lower Broadway rather than go home. He would send Ida telegrams apologizing for his behavior and sign them, "Unfortunately for you, your husband Ben" (Abbott, 2013). Unlike Ben, Ida had a knack for hanging onto money. It was rumored that she did not complain about his gambling habit, but that Ben paid her half of his winnings and if he lost he had to take the loss himself or pay her for her time waiting for him. If he needed to borrow money, she charged him interest (Cox, 1964, pp. 97–98). By 1897, Ben was in serious debt, close to bankruptcy. Ida gave him the money needed to settle his debt, but in return she requested that he sell her his controlling shares in the newspaper. Ben died in 1900 with few assets because everything he owned was in Ida's name (Cox, 1964, p. 100).

Ida was said to have a hobby of her own. According to the *Boston Globe*, her hobby was the stock market, which she credited with building her fortune with the help of Frank Work, her handsome broker and agent; they studied the reports daily ("Rich Recluse," 1931, p. A44). The same article in the *Globe* stated that Ida lost interest in wearing dresses and jewelry when she was 30 and turned to the stock market as a hobby after her husband died—it was a profitable hobby.

However, Ida had little knowledge of how to run a newspaper. Within a year after the death of her husband, the newspaper was run into the ground by her mismanagement. In 1901, she received an offer from Frank Munsey of $340,000 to buy the failing paper. Ida accepted the offer but on the condition that the money be brought to her in new $1,000 bills. According to the 1931 article "After Fortune," Munsey's assistant handed each bill, one by one, to Ida, who immediately inspected them and quickly passed the bills to her sister Mary, her daughter Emma, and even the hotel manager to examine them as well. The sum was noted paid when all had nodded approval.

The Panic of 1907, which caused a run on banks, exacerbated Ida's fear of being poor. She demanded all of her money from the bank in cash (Abbott, 2013). At the time she withdrew all of her money from the bank, it was discovered that she had also sold furniture, oil paintings, sculptures, tapestries, and other valuable objects that she acquired during her marriage to Benjamin Wood. "She had done well with her years. More than a million dollars were hers to do with what she wished. She was determined that none of it would slip through her hands" (McKnaught, 1932, p. A54). Ida went into a panic when a run on banks became front-page news, she became increasingly paranoid that people were going to rob her, so she withdrew from the life she had lived in the public eye into her suite at the Herald Square, never to be seen again.

Emma, Mary, and Ida all lived together as recluses in squalor in a two-room suite (rooms 551–552) at the Herald Square Hotel, rented originally by Mary. The length of their stay at the hotel was from 1907 to 1932. "They never left their suite; hotel staff fetched food (evaporated milk, coffee, crackers, bacon, eggs and an occasional fish), as well as Cuban cigars" ("The Strange Story," 2013). The three women cooked their own meals and rarely ventured outside. The 273-room Herald Square Hotel was built in 1898, and like Ida, was once grand and opulent. However, over the years the hotel had been squeezed out by an ever-growing and changing society and was marked for the wrecking ball. "Now the hotel and Ida were dying together" (Cox, 1964, p. 3).

For 24 years, Ida never ventured outside of her suite. "It was reported that Ida was in a state of ignorance about everything that had happened in the world for the past twenty-odd years, and consequently had never heard a radio, or looked at a talking motion picture, or flown in an airplane" (Cox, 1964, p. 44). Ida told reporters that she believed they were lying about airplanes. She portrayed herself to the hotel staff as poor. Whenever the staff of the hotel brought up the groceries, she told them that the money she was giving them was the last she had and she didn't know what she was going to do when it all ran out (p. 9). She always tipped them a dime for their service.

When Mary took sick, Ida questioned the doctor about his fee for the house call before she would even let him enter the suite, and when she was told of Mary's death, her response was "Now she'll have to be buried, and that will cost money" (p. 8). The hotel called and sent numerous messages for the rent money, and every time the women paid their bill in cash.

Emma died in 1928 at the age of 71 and Mary died in 1931 at the age of 91; neither ever married or had children. Both women's funerals were presided over by Father Gregor, and both were buried from the same church with no one in attendance and no flowers, cards, or telegrams. Ida did not attend either funeral (Cox, 1964, p. 18).

After Emma and Mary passed, Ida was left alone without anyone looking after her affairs. In 1931, Ida was 93 years old, nearly blind, partially deaf, feeble, and bent over like a question mark. "She had refused medical and legal advice and almost starved herself by cooking meager meals over a gas burner" ("Mrs Ida Wood," 1937, p. A9). Onlookers said she weighed approximately 70 pounds and was emaciated. Toast and condensed milk were her daily diet and she lived on pennies a day, in constant fear that someone would rob her. Ida began refusing to open the door to her apartment, even if it was the bellman bringing her the food she ordered from him. She would command him to toss it over the transom. Ida increasingly became reclusive (Wood, 2010, p. 2). Upon the death of her sister Mary, lawyers were brought in to handle the estate and funeral arrangements. At this time, Ida hinted to the lawyers that she had a good deal of money stashed in her bedroom. Due to her deteriorating health, the condition of her room at the hotel, the statements she made about large sums of cash in her place, and her combative behavior, the lawyers decided that she needed someone who could protect her interests.

On September 22, 1931, Ida was adjudged incompetent (Cox, 1964, p. 38). Due to her poor vision, ideas of persecution and paranoia, senile deterioration, and lack of an ability to care for herself, she was assigned a court-appointed guardian: Otis Wood, the son of Fernando Wood, Ida's nephew, who was believed to be her closest living relative at the time. An attorney, David Asch, stated that Ida retained large amounts of negotiable, valuable securities and money, although the exact amount could not be verified, and that she was vulnerable to anyone entering her suite and taking advantage of her deafness, blindness, and weakness (Cox, 1964, pp. 31–32).

However, contrary to what was reported in court, Ida always maintained there was nothing wrong with her, and that she was competent to handle her own affairs and would be better off if people left her alone. "Her wandering mind was sometimes in the past, sometimes in the present, but always alert, and the old habits of living were as strong as ever, even though her environment had changed" (Cox, 1964, p. 61). Otis Wood petitioned to have Ida moved to another floor in the hotel, one that was cleaner, safer, and quieter. Ida protested by sitting in her rocking chair and yelling; therefore, she was carried out covered with a blanket wrapped around her and forcibly moved to her new room.

In her new surroundings, Ida refused to eat meals if they cost more than 25 cents. The nurses who cared for her learned how to lie so she would eat. Occasionally, Ida would run to the window and yell to people below that she was being held as a prisoner. No one heard her cries (Cox, 1964, p. 61). Even in her old age, Ida still spun stories of her childhood and past:

> My mother had a very good education, you know. She spoke German, Spanish, and Italian, and she wanted me to be educated too, so she sent me to boarding school in New Orleans. My brothers never married. My poor brother Louis was drowned up in Massachusetts. It was funny how I met my husband. He came to our house when I was fifteen. My brother and I were up in a peach tree. He said: "Well I want to see the girl who could climb that tree." Then I had to come down in front of him. I knew then I'd marry that man.
>
> (Cox, 1964, p. 63)

Of course, we now know that her stories were a mixture of truth and fabrication.

Ida died on March 12, 1932: "Pneumonia took her after a heart attack had sapped her strength several days ago" ("Mrs Ida Wood," 1937, p. A9). After her death, there was a firestorm of potential "Mayfield" and "Wood" heirs coming forward to claim her fortune. The questions remained: Who was Ida Wood and who were the rightful heirs? What people knew about Ida was the public picture she projected, until she died and Joseph Cox discovered the truth of her identity.

When the doctor arrived on scene to assess Mary's medical condition, he found himself standing in a darkened room, illuminated only by a small light in the hall. When he flipped the light switch on, he found himself standing in the only clear space in the room.

> The remainder was piled high with dust-laden rubbish. Piles of magazines and papers, packages and cardboard boxes of every shape and size, hat-boxes and valises, barrels, trunks, a few wooden boxes, rolls of carpeting, bundles of what looked like yellow portieres—all were thrown together in indescribable confusion.
>
> (Cox, 1964, p. 6)

The description of the setting continues to shed light on the squalor that Ida, Emma, and Mary lived in:

> There were a few chairs in the room, but they were buried under heaping stacks of old books, magazines, and packages or correspondence tied with a ribbon and string. An ancient dilapidated rocker was the only place remaining to sit. In the one corner, barricaded by piles of bundles, was what passed for a sofa, but it was no more than a shapeless heap of old sheets, blankets, afghans, and comforters. Some of them obviously had not been washed or cleaned for years.
>
> (Cox, 1964, pp. 6–7)

As the doctor continued to survey the suite, he noticed a shelf on the wall that was littered to the ceiling; however, there was a small space that held a china cup, two small china plates, tarnished silver, a drinking cup, and a small saucepan. The doctor located the grimy, two-burner electric stove that Ida used for cooking on top of a dusty trunk. He asked where her sister Mary was. Ida led him to the other room, which he described as much the same as the first room, just as littered, but with an even dimmer bulb.

What shocked onlookers in the discovery of Ida's living conditions was that even though she portrayed herself as poor to the hotel staff, medical attendants, lawyers, and anyone who would listen, she was sitting on a million dollars inside the barely lit suite she resided in for over 24 years. She had amassed a fortune in cash, jewelry, and other items amid the squalor.

After he gained Ida's trust, the doctor was taken on a small tour of the suite. She pointed out dusty trunks and boxes that she said contained rare silks, jewels, and the finest lace from Ireland, Venice, and Spain. She indicated that a watch and diamond necklace had been stolen. There were 40 trunks in her suite and in storage that had not been opened since the days of the gold rush and contained expensive mementos and cash ("Mrs Ida Wood," 1937). When the locked trunks were opened, they were found to contain dozens of dresses, ball gowns, negligees, housecoats, bathrobes, sweaters, capes, and underwear and hats of every type. They also uncovered old newspaper clippings, notebooks, magazines, excelsior, string, bits of cloth, and small pieces of wood (Cox, 1964, pp. 42–43).

She told the doctor that even though they stole some jewelry, robbers did not get her cash. Ida indicated that she had hidden her money well, that it was $385,000 in cash, and that she sometimes forgot where she stashed it (Cox, 1964, pp. 23–24). Due to this omission by Ida, acting on consultation from lawyers, the New York Supreme Court got involved to protect her interest. What they found astonished them. Ida had hidden her cash throughout her suite, and when the trunks were opened, they were indeed full of jewelry and dresses of the style she wore when she danced with Edward VII. Ida handed over nearly $400,000 in a bundle of bills from the folds of her dress in protest, but the remainder of her stash needed to be located throughout her apartment while she slept. Ida's nurse located a money belt underneath Ida's clothes that contained bundles of cash totaling $500,000 and inside several trunks and upholstered furniture in her apartment were jewelry and gems appraised at $900,000 ("After Fortune," 1931).

Reports indicate that money was found in various places around her suite, including in pots and pans. A $40,000 diamond necklace was found in a cracker box surrounded by moldy crackers; in various shoeboxes were yellowed stocks and bonds worth tens of thousands of dollars with interest and dividend coupons that had not been redeemed in decades (Wood, 2010, p. 3). Ida liked railroad bonds best, and she had considerable railroad holdings when the boom days came to the Middle West ("Rich Recluse," 1931). She was found to have 11 certificates of Union Pacific preferred stock and a $10,000 registered first-mortgage land grant Union Pacific bond. "The certificates were for 1,020 shares of preferred stock, some in Ida's name, others in Mary's" (Cox, 1964, p. 25). Cox continues that later in the day, Ida brought out additional coupons she had cut from bonds totaling $50,000 in negotiable first-mortgage Union Pacific bonds. She handed a bundle to one of the men who was searching her suite for cash. He pulled the string and out came a $500 Lincoln gold note, a $100 bank note, and additional Union Pacific bonds worth $95,000 (Cox, 1964, p. 26). Notably, the cash that was found in Ida's suite dated back to the Civil War days (50 years), and many of the bills were faded and moldy. The *Washington Post* reported that she pulled out $50,000 in bonds from a sugar bag under her mattress and on another occasion pulled $5,000 from a pocket in her dress ("Aged Recluse," 1931). "Under her protesting eyes and in spite of grumbling words, a search of her belongings unearthed nearly $1,000,000 in moldy currency and coin, an equal amount in jewels and invaluable mementos (including a gold-headed ebony cane President Monroe gave her father-in-law) of an intriguing past" ("Mrs Ida Wood," 1937, p. A9).

Due to Ida's mental status and the amount of cash that was discovered in her room, there was a frenzy to locate additional money or jewels that Ida might have misplaced. The body of her sister Mary was even exhumed from its grave to see if Ida had hidden money in the coffin, but none was found (Abbott, 2013).

Ida's original suite at Herald Square was completely turned upside down; all furniture was methodically taken apart, clothes sliced open, perfume and cologne bottles emptied, mattresses gutted, carpet rolled up, and the plumbing in the suite taken apart to check drains and pipes for valuables. No other valuables were found, but they did find 5,000 pieces of soap, gathered from all over the world, most still in their original wrappers (Cox, 1964, p. 47). When some of the trunks were opened, even more soap cakes were found.

Additionally, searchers found dusty portraits and photographs from her life with Ben, bundles of Ben and Ida's letters to each other, daguerreotypes, pounds of crumbling *Daily News* business stationery, huge batches of keys that did not go to the trunks, several balls of string, rolls of wrapping paper, and several bolts of linen toweling. In another trunk was Bohemian glass that had been blown specific for Ida, lace in its original boxes from Bonnet et Cie in Lyon, dresses that had never been worn, capes of gold and silver material, and dozens of dinner menus (Cox, 1964, p. 50).

When the search of Ida's suite, storage, and personal belongings was completed, what would become of all this matter would be settled in court. Originally, 1,103 supposed descendants from the "Mayfield" and "Wood" families came forward to stake claims on Ida's estate (Cox, 1964, p. 177). However, after Ida's true identity was proven, there were only 10 Walsh heirs that rightfully shared in the fortune. Out of the 10 descendants, none had ever met Ida, nor did they even know of her existence (Cox, 1964, p. 225). This woman was so secretive that even her heirs were unaware of her life.

Personal thoughts

After reading about and attending to the voices of the six individuals selected, I found it fitting to provide my own meaningful experience, having had a chance to be present to the language of images, metaphors, myths, and symbols that revealed themselves. The soul language spoke to me by honoring the fluidity of their stories.

As I, the reader, sit with my thoughts and spend time in the company of the Beales' life stories, aloneness and emptiness are the feelings I keep coming back to. Sadness and unmet dreams that never came to fruition are evident in the house and hoard that the Beales lived with. They filled themselves up with the unconditional love of cats and objects instead of pursuing intimate relationships with others because it was safer than risking being hurt or disappointed. I wonder about the pain, sorrow, and sadness that were downplayed in the two movies or omitted in the written documents detailing their lives. Even though the movies about the Beales depicted two women who were joyful, sang and danced, and seemed to have a positive view of their lives, I pondered what was not being said—the look in their eyes when the camera came in for a close-up that seemed to tell a story all its own. Occasionally, the camera caught a glimpse of a pending thought, a peculiar glance, or a tear in their eyes, but nothing was said. No one asked them to describe the uncomfortable feeling projected into the room. The camera just sat on the moment for a few seconds, stillness in the air, and with grace the next scene began.

I see the murkiness and deadness that surrounded them and I sense this is the essence of their story: the death and decay of two women whose lives were not lived according to their hopes and dreams. The dead vines that covered Grey Gardens were signifiers of death moving in, surrounding them, holding them prisoner in a world that had swallowed them up, killing their spirits.

Reflecting back on the life story of the Collyer brothers, I feel like they tried to hide from everything they feared, especially outsiders and change. They built an elaborate fortress to keep these things from impinging on their private lives. As I sit with the numerous pictures depicting their hoard, feelings of being over-whelmed and intense fear arise for me. I wonder if this is a projection of what the brothers must have been feeling—overwhelmed in their situation with their objects and Homer's medical issues and intense fear of the neighborhood closing in on them.

A collection of beauty and trash was stashed in their hoard. To me, this resembles the ever-changing cycle of life, the degeneration that humans go through. Holding onto something beautiful and fearing it will be taken from you, to me, is synonymous with holding onto our youth. The more we fear that we have no control over losing something, the more neurotic we become in trying to hold onto it. I wonder if this was not the conundrum that the Collyer brothers found themselves in: trying to hold onto something beautiful, their past, and fearful of losing it.

After spending time in the research with Andy Warhol, I can't help but contemplate the complex way this man presented himself to the public. I am struck by his level of desire to be famous and recognized for his uniqueness, and his intense longing to be remembered for his artwork. I think he achieved his lifelong goal of being famous, even after death, not only for his art but also through the materials he hoarded. The contents of the 610 boxes were just as complex, unique, shocking, and obtuse as he was while he was alive. The time capsules became a catalog of his daily life, a way to be remembered and still shock onlookers. Andy hoarded the minutiae and trivial details of his own life. He seemed to live by his statement about how the mind makes spaces into spaces, and as a person ages more spaces and compartments are created, leaving room to put more things into the compart-ments. I am curious about what images and metaphors are being unconsciously projected that reveal painful revelations about Andy Warhol. The items hoarded, from his personal medications and prescriptions to his collection of fan mail, show symbolically his ego in crisis searching for a literal way to identify himself.

Andy stated that "publicity is like peanuts, once you start you can't stop" (Warhol, 1975, p. 94). I believe Andy lived his whole life under this principle: his work, his art, and his collection of items never stopped. To Andy everything was art and everything was important; nothing was too small or insignificant. He wanted to be important, a living artwork, and he achieved just that. However, I pondered the things that Andy kept to himself, the sides he didn't share with others, and in what ways the objects he hoarded and the rituals he attended to speak volumes about the man he was, insecurities included.

As the reader, *old*, *dark*, and *dingy* are words that come to mind when I think of the story of Ida Wood. When I received the book *The Recluse of Herald Square* in the mail, I pondered the significance it bore—the book itself was old, dingy, and falling apart at the seams. The copy I ordered once belonged to the Derbyshire County Council Libraries and Heritage, and it must have passed through a thousand hands before it got to mine, giving me an opportunity to now tell its story. It makes me wonder how many hands Ida's money and objects passed through before reaching Joseph Cox, who eventually told their story.

The tension of the opposites portrayed in Ida's story is what stands out for me: life and death, light and dark, rich and poor. The glamour of the life Ida lived— ballroom dances, royalty, fine dining, and traveling—contrasted so dramatically with the squalor, darkness, and solitude that surrounded her once she removed herself from the elite social circle. In my imagination, I ponder the untold story of three women who exiled themselves for 24 years in a two-room suite that was barely lit. There is so much unknown about their journey, just like the book, which inevitably told an incomplete story that left me puzzled and curious. Ida went to great lengths to deny her family of origin and her previous identity, repressing the feelings of shame and not allowing deep emotions to surface. Her hoarding experience seems to be a direct reflection of her unconscious conflict dealing with a shameful identity, repressed into repetitive behaviors of acquiring money and jewelry, which she adopted as her identity. Maybe that is how Ida wanted to be remembered.

In an attempt to avoid her fears, she built her hoard, which created feelings of safety, identity, and opportunity; however, this was a false defense that was implemented to protect her fragile ego from further pain. In my reflection on Ida's story, her fear and vulnerability are masked by an outward appearance of control, but her inward suffering has rendered her helpless to manage her relationships and objects. I was sad to read that she did not attend the funeral of either Emma or Mary. By not attending, she avoided the outward appearance of the feeling of grief, which would possibly have been unpleasant. It is apparent that Ida tried to mitigate and avoid suffering through the accumulation of her objects, but then she suffered from a pseudo problem and its symptoms.

The deaths of loved ones were recurrent in Ida's story; however, the pain of mourning and the scars grief leaves behind seemed to be missing. I wonder if her identification with particular objects stored in her trunks was due to a fragmented and incomplete process of healthy mourning, an autonomous force bigger than herself. When hoarders search for a reason for their pain, it is not from a place of understanding, but sought through a catharsis, which can be told through the images of their objects.

In conclusion, these reflections were offered after several months of being present and attuned to the voices spoken in the text and the images, metaphors, and symbols that emerged from the readings, and after completing the fusion on general structure. Being a witness to all the material presented still allows for a spirit of invitation and wonderment at the experience of being present with each historical figure, which adds support to the findings in this chapter.

8
THEMES IDENTIFIED WITH HOARDERS

After close evaluation of the material presented in the previous section, I discovered four themes that revealed themselves in all six historical figures' stories. The four themes, along with supporting examples from the figures' biographies, will be presented in this section, as well as an exploration of the structure that binds together the fundamental themes seen with each historical figure.

Loss

Loss is a profound emotional process for everyone; it crosses cultural and gender lines. Loss can be physical, as in the death of a loved one, loss of good health from an illness, or loss of a person or thing through abandonment. All three types of loss can be seen in the stories of the historical figures presented.

Both Homer and Langley Collyer experienced loss to various degrees through-out their lifetimes. In their biographies, four losses consistently surfaced:

1   Their sister died as an infant, before they were born. This loss would have been felt by the family as a whole, even though the brothers were not born yet.
2   An additional loss for both brothers was felt when their father "abandoned his family" in 1919 and moved to another residence, visiting his family often but not residing with the brothers and their mother.
3   The brothers lost both parents: their father in 1923 and their mother 6 years later. The brothers were especially close to their mother.
4   Homer lost his eyesight and his health deteriorated, creating a need to be cared for by his brother Langley.

Edith and Little Edie Beale faced loss as well; their attempts to cope with their loss united the pair in their grief. In their biographies, eight significant losses were identified:

1   Edie had a reoccurring respiratory illness that plagued her as a child, keeping her home from school and in bed for days and weeks at a time with acute respiratory illness.
2   Edith experienced a profound loss when Phelan left her and married his secretary. The divorce was very difficult for Edith emotionally.
3   The breakup of Edie's first love with Julius Krug was a significant loss for her.
4   Edie's ideals of one day getting married and finding her true love never came to fruition.
5   Edith's lover (after her divorce) ended their relationship as well. He moved out of her residence, leaving her alone.
6   The loss of Edie's hair to alopecia was traumatic for her.
7   For both, the death of Phelan was experienced as a loss.
8   After Phelan died, both Edith and Edie lost the income they relied on to pay for their lifestyles at Grey Gardens.

Andy Warhol experienced his own losses as well during the course of his life. His biography tells of the various losses he had to cope with. Four noteworthy ones were identified:

1   Andy's illness as a child created a loss because he was not able to attend school over a year and had to stay indoors resting, which in turn created the loss of a social environment that could mitigate feelings of isolation and loneliness.
2   The death of Andy's father when he was 13 years old was a traumatic loss.
3   He experienced numerous losses when intimate relationships ended due to his awkwardness.
4   After being shot, Andy suffered a loss of security. He reported that this event forever changed the way he perceived his health and mortality.

Ida Mayfield Wood was no stranger to loss as well:

1   Six of her siblings died as infants, two before Ida was born and four after.
2   Another sibling, Louis, died at age 13 by drowning. Ida had his body exhumed and moved it to New York to be buried at the family plot.
3   Her father left her mother and moved to California, leaving her mother and siblings alone. She eventually moved them to New York.
4   Her father died unexpectedly in California.
5   Her mother died suddenly while on a trip back to their country to visit family. Ida had her body flown back to New York for burial.
6   The loss of stability and infrastructure of banks in 1907 created a fear of losing money for Ida.

Shame

A person's identity and view of self can promote or hinder his or her adaptation to the environment and social norms. Feelings of not being good enough, not measuring up, and embarrassment about past history or origins were all evident in the historical figures' biographies, as were feelings of shyness, humiliation, and inadequacy. Both external shame by others and internal shame within one's self were significant conditions in each of their lives.

Homer and Langley Collyer's history embodied shame in various forms, both externally from the residents in Harlem and internally through their own perceived ideals.

1   They were dishonest about their origin: they stated their ancestors came to America on the *Speedwell*, but in fact they arrived in America 52 years after the *Mayflower*.
2   Langley felt as if he was not good enough musically because Paderewski received better notices than he did.
3   Both brothers were teased by the neighborhood kids and called names like "ghosty men" and "spooks." A sign was posted on their house stating it was a ghost house.
4   Homer was unable to care for himself and relied on Langley's help to conduct his daily life.

For Edith and Little Edie Beale, shame was present in many of the same contexts as it was for the Collyer brothers:

1   Edith and Edie were not supported in following their dreams of becoming a singer and actress. Both of their fathers put down their talents as a waste of their time.
2   Edie's alopecia made her insecure about her appearance.
3   Neighbors and outsiders ridiculed the way the Beales lived.

Andy Warhol suffered greatly from his own internal shame.

1   Andy came from a poor immigrant family who lived in the slums of Pittsburgh.
2   He was ridiculed in school because his hands shook as a side effect of his illness.
3   His family made fun of him and nicknamed him "Red Nose Warhola."
4   Andy was embarrassed by his appearance, notably his acne and red nose.

The central theme in Ida Mayfield Wood's story is the shame she felt regarding her familial origins. Ida went to great lengths to hide her Irish background and create a fantasy upbringing with a more prominent background.

1   Ida was dishonest about her upbringing and her background growing up in Massachusetts, not New York. She was from a poor Irish immigrant family.

2   She pretended that her sister was her daughter and hid her identity from outsiders.

Object clusters

A notable trait among the historical figures researched was the propensity to hoard objects similar in classification and function. Each person accumulated objects particular to past interests, hobbies, or history, and each one seemed to collect numerous versions of particular objects. These valued objects are mirrors of each subject's personal myth; hoarding is a form of myth-making and myth amplifying through imagination and lifestyle, which allows an individual's myth to come alive.

Homer and Langley Collyer both had a love for singing and playing musical instruments. Their father Herman was a prominent doctor who loved medicine. In their collection of items discovered after their death, numerous object clusters were found.

1   Fourteen pianos and five violins were found in the hoard along with an accordion, a trombone, a clavichord, a cornet, sheet music, and an opera program.
2   Different types of medical equipment were found amid the junk, including a glass static machine, disassembled medical specimens, an X-ray machine, a machine to treat rheumatism, and a 2,500-volume medical library.
3   Expensive home decoration items were also found, such as tapestries, Victorian oil lamps and vases, 13 Oriental rugs, oil paintings, fine linens, silks, wools, damask, brocade, and dressmaking dummies that belonged to their mother Susie.
4   Numerous weapons were located inside the home as well: three revolvers, two rifles, a shotgun, ammunition, a bayonet, and a saber.

The object clusters for the Beales seemed to constellate around heirlooms from their glamorous high society past and their current hobby of breeding cats.

1   The living room and dining room was the central locale for most of the dusty, antique furniture and a grand piano. Also found were a large oil painting of a once young and vibrant Edith Beale and a letter from Phelan written on their wedding day. These two items were kept in the bedroom, in close proximity to Edith.
2   Edith and Edie bred over 300 cats and had numerous raccoons that they fed on a daily schedule.
3   Due to their hobby of breeding cats, the most hoarded item found in Grey Gardens was empty cat food cans. In the dining room alone, there was a 5-foot-high pile of empty cans.

Of particular interest is what objects presented themselves for Andy Warhol's hoard. He had an extensive collection of items that resonated on various themes.

Andy's clusters of objects seemed to center around celebrities, his fame, art, and items that brought him joy.

1   Andy had a fondness for perfume bottles; he had an extensive collection of half full containers.
2   An extensive collection of biscuit jars was found in his possession.
3   He had a collection of 1,659 items of pottery, 72 Navajo blankets, and art deco furniture.
4   There were 33 pieces of artwork by various artists.
5   Tickets, flyers, invitations, and posters to parties and events were located among his items.
6   Numerous notes, cards, and pictures addressed to Andy from fans and celebrities were discovered.
7   The time capsules themselves can be seen as cluster objects; he hoarded 570 cardboard boxes full of objects that defined his life.

Ida Mayfield Wood's hobby was playing the stock market—making money, which in turn created what she believed was an identity of stature. Additionally, her social status was very important to her, as was making a name for herself in New York's high society.

1   Money was the most hoarded object found among Ida's possessions. Old currency and coins in small denominations were found throughout her suite, totaling over a million dollars.
2   She also collected soap cakes from all around the world; over 5,000 pieces were discovered in both her suite and her storage.
3   Numerous pieces of jewelry and loose gems were hidden throughout her suite, totaling $900,000 in value.
4   Dusty portraits, photographs, and hundreds of letters between her and her husband Ben were hoarded.
5   Expensive dresses and imported lace from Ireland, Venice, and Spain were collected and stored inside trunks in her suite.
6   The 40 trunks that Ida used to store her items from the past can be seen as an object cluster as well.

Shadow inhabiting setting

The most prevalent theme that emerged for all six historical figures was the unconscious projection of each individual's shadow into his or her setting. The unfavorable characteristics of each person were projected into their habitat and came alive in the darkness and murkiness of their surroundings. Death moved into each one of their dwellings, mirroring the inward experience one feels when soul dies. Through embarrassment, shame, fear, and the rejection and judgment of onlookers, they withdrew inward, avoiding facing life and its perceived threats by creating an illusory identity and setting of safety.

Homer and Langley Collyer felt like prisoners in their own home, and their setting became a reflection of their inward fear, a prison or fortress on lockdown. The beauty of the home and numerous ornate objects still shone through the dust and decay of the mansion: a likeness of lives once lived by the Collyer family. However, the mansion sat in disrepair and brokenness, a reflection of the lives of Homer and Langley.

Decay, isolation, emptiness, and brokenness also describe the Beales' lives and their setting. Grey Gardens was described as having mostly empty rooms, decaying floorboards and ceilings, and rotting food throughout. Additionally, the decline in the beauty of Grey Gardens mirrored the Beales' descent from high society into isolation. The lasting image of Grey Gardens shows it with dead vines strangling the once vibrant-colored home into a grey lifeless dwelling—a striking parallel to the life the Beales ended up living.

Andy Warhol's setting was different from the previous two examples. His hoarding, for the most part, was confined to items discarded into cardboard boxes. However, one can still see how his inward turmoil, chaos, and insecurities are reflected in the contents of the boxes. There were over 200,000 items stored in hundreds of boxes that imitated fears, death, and decay, all descriptive words that describe Andy in some fashion. From the dead bees and mummified foot found in his boxes to the decaying birthday cake, pizza dough, acne medication, and prescriptions, one can see how his life mirrored the contents of his hoard.

Andy struggled with self-ambivalence and uncertainty about himself, his art, and his fame. His acquiring and accumulation of random objects was an attempt to strengthen his certainty about his self-worth and give him a sense of security. He wanted to be important and valued by others; therefore, he felt all of his items had importance and value. Additionally, he had a commitment to a vision of art that embraced the mundane, as if it were an attempt to raise what he found commonplace about his own background to a higher aesthetic level. In this sense, it could be seen as a redemptive act to transform the random and trivial effects of his life into compartmentalized moments of artistic consciousness.

Lies, secrecy, and fear of discovery seemed to dominate Ida Mayfield Wood's adult life. Due to her fears, Ida isolated herself in her suite; over time her fears turned to paranoia. Her setting was a direct reflection of her fears: she was afraid of running out of money and being robbed, therefore, she lived in a barely lit room, scarcely ate, and hid her possessions throughout her suite. She hid the secret of her wealth by being a recluse and lying to hotel staff, insisting that she was poor and that her money was running out.

9

BURYING EMOTIONS WITH OBJECTS

Soul (or a psychological experience) expresses loss in longing: a longing to retrieve what once was cherished and now is lost. When soul does not receive back what it has perceived as loss, a death can occur, activating a complex or wounding. Once activated, the wounding can be seen through hoarding tendencies. The individual creates an intense personal relationship with an object or objects possessed. The individual possesses the object, which is never to be abandoned but kept securely placed within the home. To the hoarder, the object comes *alive* with feelings and in need of love. Confusing their possessions with their emotions is common among hoarders.

The descriptive language used by individuals who hoard is full of metaphors, images, and poetic reverie and includes feelings of safety, connection, and love. One example is that a cookbook isn't just a book full of recipes: it represents a good cook, a well-informed person, a responsible mother/father, or a connection to a loved one who cooked. Similarly, travel brochures represent unrealistic future travel plans, memories of a trip taken, or a bond with a loved one who traveled often. Objects hoarded carry a unique significance to the person who cherishes them. The utility, waste, and responsibility of an object are different depending on the life experiences of the individual and the unconscious conflicts and feelings that remain unprocessed.

When individuals enter into an intense experience with the objects they possess, the objects become part of a larger identity for them, creating the illusion of a more meaningful life that is full of potential. Allowing an object to encompass a fantasy of a life once lived or the degeneration of a dream becomes the integral process of identity for a hoarder, mementoes on a large scale. Memories, a sense of self, nostalgia, shame, and loss are often intertwined into the objects hoarded; the individuals meet their shadows in the decaying and death of their setting, raising deeper reflections of a life not lived, or a life lived in caring for these items, putting them to bed in boxes or tucked neatly in the corners of their houses. They find their identities mirrored in the setting and objects hoarded, while the setting and objects reveal aspects of their identities that were previously unfamiliar and unconscious.

Deepening the understanding of self and psyche through engagement in setting and objects collected allows for learning and discovery for individuals struggling with hoarding tendencies. Even though none of the historical figures chosen for this book had an opportunity to learn from what and how they hoarded, nor did their hoarding confirm their known identities; retrospectively their intense experiences with hoarding revealed the depth and breadth of their emotional lives, and the soul's struggle to be alive. Soul demands growth. When a hoarder holds an object captive for the sake of love and connection, he or she is held captive as well, stifling growth. Life is to be endured through many deaths, many losses, and enlargement through suffering; however, hoarders fear the intense emotions that encompass this transformative journey. Transformation requires the loss of stasis, and hoarders cannot endure the suffering of further loss. Therefore, reverting to defenses and coping through hoarding inevitably keeps the individual from experiencing this type of growth.

The thematic image of death inhabiting an individual's setting is fascinating. The imagination of the hoarder yields surprising insight into the significance of acquiring things, then developing and maintaining a regimen of living with them, even the dark, murky, and molded remnants of things. Even the decay itself can be seen as a life force that comforts.

The image of the dead vines holding Grey Gardens in an embrace is a remarkable example of how death consumed not only the dwelling but also the souls of the individuals who inhabited the space. The videos and photographs conveyed the sorrow and sadness that Edith and Edie endured throughout their lives and how they buried themselves in emotional, psychic, and physical clutter. Psyche and self vividly and potently presented themselves in the images of their decaying setting and in the objects they acquired. In the filming of *Grey Gardens*, the filmmakers captured raw emotions from the Beales that are seldom seen with hoarders due to their isolation. They attempted to allow for the embracing of painful revelations, increasing consciousness for the Beales. However, the lens was met with rejection when Edith told them to turn the camera off, avoiding her own pain and suffering.

People who hoard crave an emotional connection. In our misguided attempts to help them clean their settings, collectively we fail them, and it should be no surprise that they journey deeper into reclusiveness to find a truer sense through a connection with their objects.

Death and decay appeared in all six historical figures' stories in some fashion, whether in their actual dwellings or in the objects they hoarded. It was fascinating to see the connection between shame and decay, where the theme manifested itself, and where shame beckoned each one of them in their journeys to hoarding. Shameful experiences are sometimes too overwhelming for individuals to handle and process. Consequently, people who hoard employ alternative emotional strategies to cope in order to prevent the breakdown of the self. Knowing that individuals prefer not to experience shame, devising alternative mechanisms of handling shame-prone situations could lead to other emotional substitutions. There is a deep curiosity about whether shame is the catalyst that allows an individual's hoarded treasure to become the grotesque. The level of shame individuals have experienced guides the regulation of closeness in their intimate relationships; however, the same types of emotions regulate closeness with their objects. Feeling rejected by loved ones fuels hoarders' need for attachment through objects that will never abandon them, even in decay.

The physical world of material objects is in stark contrast to the pull of the imaginal world, which makes itself available to the bizarre and rotting symbolism of one person's treasure. As clinical psychology preoccupies itself with diagnosing and prescribing a fixed treatment regimen for the condition of hoarding, collectively we overlook the persuasive force of fantasy and how hoarders idealize objects to avoid real pain. Instead of seeing the condition of hoarding as an atypical attachment to inanimate objects that are accumulated, we need to focus on the symbolic roles that objects play for these individuals. Seeing hoarders for their unique individuality and being witnesses to their stories and the symbolism in their objects can bring to conscious awareness their repressed feelings of pain and loss.

Seeing what the objects represent for each individual encapsulates the essence of the experience for them. The perceived ambivalence of the items Andy Warhol hoarded brought about subjectivity about whether or not the items meant anything to him at all. Consequently, what emerged was that this peculiar behavior of his inadvertently played out to minimize abandonment, to relieve his pain.

Warhol captivated onlookers by what he chose to hoard: nail clippings, dead bees, pizza dough, and birthday cake. These objects represented critical parts of his identity and symbolized a frustrated attempt to renew the symbolic function missing in his life. Collectively, we attempt to find symbolic meaning in our lives, and our physical world becomes a mirror as metaphor for our internal world. Warhol's inward chaos was directly reflected in the 200,000 items catalogued from his collection, and they served a symbolic function of creating the iconic identity of this man after his death. There might have been inward chaos in Andy's insistence on preserving and cataloguing the incidental effects of his life, but there was also a refusal to regard anything as worthless or devoid of meaning. Even though Andy put his items away in boxes and labeled them, the chaos that these 610 boxes created after his death was astonishing. This was a defense against a deeper fear that Andy himself was a being without worth or meaning. Do we all find unique ways to fight off that same fear of chaos as a void if we dig deeper into our shadow?

Whether we know it or not, something larger than ourselves is directing our steps in our personal and collective journeys. Loss has the greatest impact on individuals as a whole. There is a sense of connectedness to the story of each individual, sharing in these raw, painful, and intense moments of loss, which is rare with hoarders due to their extreme isolation. These feelings could be seen in Edith Beale's eyes when she clutched the photograph of Phelan with his enduring words of love and affirmation. Her eyes revealed her pain at the loss of their marriage and his death, and the shame she tried to hide when she demanded that the cameras be turned off. It is hard not to be deeply affected by this shared moment with a woman most have never met: a collective shared moment where her gaze is met with our gaze, sorrow met with our sorrow, to create a meaningful encounter that solidifies the phenomenon under analysis.

These individuals' stories remind us how powerful emotions can be in shaping identity and feelings of value and worth. This reality is rarely shared among hoarders due to shame, isolation, and their barriers of objects walling themselves off from others; however, there is a sense of gratefulness for the stories each historical figure left behind. They deeply shared in the inferiority that was the reality of their lives.

Loss, decay, and degeneration were part of Edith and Edie's narrative story, which was seen through the metaphors and images of the dilapidated and decayed dwelling and rotting piles of cat food. Two women surrounded by isolation and waste, were given space to share their story of loss. Homer and Langley's intense fear can be seen through the transformation of their setting into a fortress and also in the objects they hoarded, like guns and medical journals to keep Homer well. The way they held onto their past and their youth was evident in the beautiful family artifacts that they accumulated. Andy Warhol's life was dictated by intense personal shame, wanting to be famous, and rejection by others due to the nature of his artwork and his sexual identity. The items contained in his boxes contributed to his overall identity and how he wanted people to see him. Lastly, Ida Mayfield's story, told through metaphors and images of the objects she possessed, spoke of a woman who carried personal shame from her upbringing in a poor Irish immigrant family and profound loss from the numerous family deaths throughout her life. Found among her possessions were items telling of her true identity and death records of family members that she had kept hidden from outsiders, as well as her beautiful dresses, and jewelry from elaborate dances and parties in New York— all items speaking to the life Ida lived and the fantasy she created.

The phenomenon of hoarding can be seen through a more personal lens in the example of a patient in my private practice work. She is a hoarder, and I have had direct experience with her hoarding setting. When I began my relationship with her in 2011, she was a divorced mother of four grown children, three of whom still resided with her; she characterized them as dysfunctional and verbally abusive to her. Before I met my patient, she had experienced significant losses in her life: abandonment from her mother forcing her to move around a lot as a child; loss of a social environment and feelings of loneliness; the death of her grandmother, whom she considered to be a great mother figure; and divorce due to infidelity from a man she considered her soul mate. During our work together, she lost her father as well. These losses, I believe, were the catalysts driving her deeper into her hoard. At our first session, the most striking aspects of my patient were her portrayed brokenness and sadness and her verbalization of longing for intimacy after experiencing the death of her grandmother and her divorce.

When I first stepped into her home, I had not even ventured on my PhD dissertation or this book journey, nor did I know that this topic would lend itself to me for research. I still fondly remember our encounter in her home where she allowed me to be present among her items she cherished. We did not talk much, just stood in the stillness of the moment, allowing me to feel what was being projected into the room. The memory of that experience is still etched in my consciousness as a defining moment of realizing how prominent the connection between emotions and objects can be for a hoarder. Her home was large, with ornate furniture, the most beautiful I had ever seen. The large rooms were cluttered with boxes, papers, and clothes to a height of approximately 4 feet. She had a large concrete water fountain in the living room and another Buddha-inspired one in her master bedroom, but there was no water in them, only large ashtrays holding debris. I noticed numerous picture frames on her sofa table depicting perceived happier times with her kids and ex-husband, frozen and etched in her consciousness as they sat on the table and collected years' worth of dust. The smells of feces, urine, and animal dander filled the home on this August day due to the numerous cat cages stacked in the living room and the dogs that ran free on the bottom floor and backyard of the residence. The air conditioner was broken, leaving the air hot and stale, and only the front and back door could be opened for a breeze.

We had many moments of clarity among her possessions, but the objects that stood out the most for me were the inspirational verses on the walls projecting happiness, gratefulness, and the beauty of life and family. I counted at least 75 throughout the house, either hanging high up on the walls in picture frames, stuck to the walls as stickers, or sitting on her furniture as trinkets. In our eventual discussions about these verses, the patient verbalized a desire to possess these feelings inwardly, not just outwardly in her home. Additionally, I couldn't help but make a connection about how her large, expansive home and beautiful furniture matched her generous giving spirit, her strength to endure past tragedies, and her inward beauty, in contrast to the emotional chaos she endured daily from her abusive children and ex-husband. Overall, my patient verbalized a longing to feel and connect to something more than her sadness and emptiness, which she currently achieves through hoarding. This is our journey together, which is still ongoing. After 4 years of work together from a depth psychological framework, she has stopped hoarding animals, given up all but two dogs and three cats, and begun decluttering her home and completing yard and home repairs long awaiting her attention. She has verbalized awareness of the connection between her hoarded home and her abusive, unstable relationships with family and friends. She has learned to set firm boundaries with the people in her life, including her children. She continues to do the tough work of acknowledging hurt, trauma, and sadness over the losses in her life and has begun the letting-go process for healing. As of this writing, she is discarding, donating, and packing up the items in her home, and the residence is currently listed for sale, along with the family motor home, boat, and cars accumulated during her broken marriage. She has begun the process of tough love with her grown children, set boundaries, and stopped enabling their abusive treatment of her. One child has moved out, but the other two are still attempting to undermine my patient's progress due to the perceived threat of not being able to manipulate her for their benefit. She has set firm boundaries to terminate their abuse and manipulation, and expressed her hope for their success in moving out and continuing their own journeys without her enabling their dysfunctional behaviors.

Our ongoing work is to continue transforming her loneliness into a pursuit of her heart's desire and passion to regain the strength and endurance she once possessed before being suffocated by grief and loss. I resonate with a deep belief in what James Hollis wrote in his 1993 book *The Middle Passage: From Misery to Meaning in Midlife:* "One cannot begin to heal or engage one's own soulfulness without a keen appreciation of the relationship to the Self. To achieve this requires solitude, that psychic state wherein one is wholly present to oneself" (p. 101). Hollis contends that each person is called to individuate, but not all will answer the call. I continue to help my patient understand this dynamic and how to strive toward it. I am grateful for my patient's rawness and openness to her pain and feel indebted to her for what she teaches me about this sensitive and intensely personal phenomenon.

In conclusion, it is clear that all the items hoarded are part of a hoarder's narrative identity. I question why, as mental health professionals, we choose not to connect with these individuals on a soul level, looking for meaning instead of symptoms to treat. We gain nothing by prescribing a fixed treatment regimen instead of an ensouled connection with each other, and we lose considerable insight into soul and psyche. Meeting them on a level of psyche, instead of from a clinical perspective, would provide this type of connection. Creating space for inquiry instead of formulating judgment and providing guidance and reassurance for them to explore their symbolism and desire for objects can facilitate long-term healing, more so than conventional clinical interventions.

10

SOUL WORK TOWARD RECOVERY

This book posed the question: In considering hoarding behaviors from a depth perspective, one is compelled to ask, "What does soul want in this cluttered and murky setting?" An ensouled language was sought by transforming the written word from analysis to translation and allowing what was obscure and clinical in its meaning to be a guide to the ways of psyche and soul searching. The six historical figures were understood not just from a place of knowledge, but from a sensitivity to their experience, and from hearing the text, not bombarding or assaulting the text with questions.

The intention of this book was to illuminate what is missing in clinical research about the disorder of hoarding by approaching the experience from a depth psychological expression of individuals' stories and not their pathology. From a depth psychological perspective, the lived experiences of individuals and their core schemas of value, worth, and personal identity have a direct connection to excessive acquisition of objects and the condition of hoarding. The roadmap for this book was to explore particular meanings that emerged from the figures' stories, rather than simply focusing on historical details. I believe this roadmap encouraged the revelation of soulful stirrings of the historical figures' psyches. Six core concepts were identified that evoked reflection and insight: hoarding as a disorder; perspectives on treatment; objects and meaning; making shame with clutter, loss and attachment to clutter; and diagnosis versus soul work.

The foundation of the relationship is laid with the definition of hoarding provided by Frost, Steketee, Tolin, and Renaud (2008): "Compulsive hoarding consists of the acquisition of, and failure to discard, large numbers of material possessions resulting in clutter severe enough to cause emotional distress, impair functioning, and preclude the use of living spaces for their intended purposes" (p. 193). All six historical figures examined here were unable to use their living spaces for the intended purpose due to their failure to discard their material possessions. The Beales functioned in one room of their two-story house, cooking meals on a two-burner stove next to the bed Edith slept in, and their bathroom was not usable due to a lack of running water and a broken bathtub. The Collyer brothers endured the same type of living conditions, inhabiting one room of their two-story brownstone; the living rooms and dining rooms were cluttered floor-to-ceiling, making it impossible to move through or even sit in those rooms. There was no running water in the brownstone and they were forced to obtain water from a public fountain four blocks from their home. Only one room and one bathroom were habitable in Andy Warhol's four-story Manhattan townhome; the rest of the space was littered with shopping bags, clothes, and antiques. In Ida's home, there was only one clear space to stand in the living room; the remainder was piled high with dust-laden rubbish. For cooking, she used a two-burner stove that sat atop an old trunk.

According to the Oxford English Dictionary, the etymology of *hoarding* traces back to the Old Saxon *hord*, meaning "treasure, hidden inmost place," which was how the six individuals described their possessions and how they stored them: in hiding places. Ida hid her money and jewelry in trunks throughout her apartment. Andy stored his treasure in boxes that were labeled and stored; the Collyer brothers booby-trapped their brownstone to hide their treasure from robbers; and the Beales constantly locked all doors behind themselves, both when they were home and when they went out, in order to keep intruders from stealing their possessions.

The next journey in the deepening of the relationship between object and person is to notice how perspectives on treatment can affect how individuals feel about their condition. Kalsched (1996) cites Winnicott, who believes that frequent traumatic anxiety can foreclose a transitional space for a person with hoarding problems, replacing creative imagination with fantasy to avoid the anxiety felt (p. 35). It is interesting to note how each individual suffered different types of anxious behaviors and how they attempted to avoid their pain through fantasying and idealizing objects. The Beales often verbalized their fear and paranoia of intruders and idealized their love relationship with their cats, saying they wanted to breed the cats and Edie wanted to elope with them. Andy Warhol suffered from social phobias due to his appearance, which led to anxious behaviors; through acquiring an enormous number of items, he was able to idealize his collection as having value and worth, enough to fill up and store 610 boxes over many years of collecting. The Collyer brothers engaged in paranoid behaviors, even boarding up and booby-trapping their home to keep out intruders who might want to steal their valuables; such a belief created deeper isolation for them. Ida Wood's story was strikingly similar: paranoid about being penniless and robbed of her money, she became a recluse, idealizing objects for their perceived value and hiding them throughout her apartment.

The traditional psychological perspective keeps the hoarder from being seen because it yields a fixed idea about personality and pathology. This book has illuminated how each individual's story was unique; their struggles and attempts to find meaning in their lives all moved in unique ways. When a fixed cure is produced by using a clinical modality, it is imposed on all individuals who hoard, and their unique stories are not taken into account, which can lead to resistance and further isolation. Hillman (1975) summed up this process: "And so we must free the vision of the psyche from the narrow biases of modern psychology, thereby enabling the psyche to perceive itself—its relations, its realities, its pathologies—altogether apart from psychology's modern perspective" (p. 3). By allowing each historical figure to have and to express his or her own story, voice, and experiences without imposing fixed knowledge of the problem and attempting to cure, space was opened for the imaginal to be present; a deeper exploration of objects rather than symptoms then was allowed to become central to the study.

As the relationship between object and person blossomed further, what became of particular interest was the meaning that stored itself in the objects hoarded. Myth has a large presence in directing our steps on our own journeys and helping us know what to live by; individuals have symbol-making propensities that are inherent in their objects. Bond (1993) eloquently stated this: "Something on the inside, a piece of myself, is perceived on the outside—projected onto an object" (p. 7). Imagination and lifestyle are where myth comes alive, and myth is what assigns our life meaning. It allows for individual moments in a person's life to transform into a story. This book explored the personal myth and symbolism surrounding each historical figure to see their condition more emblematically.

The inherent symbolism within the personal myth of the Beales was wrapped in the murkiness and death that surrounded them like the dead vines that covered Grey Gardens. The vines symbolized death moving in, surrounding them, and holding them prisoner in a world that had swallowed them up, killing their spirits. The death and decay of two women who did not live according to their hopes and dreams were projected into the objects they hoarded.

The Collyer brothers' inherent symbolism and personal myth seemed to focus on their feelings of being overwhelmed in their situation with their objects, Homer's medical issues, and their intense fear of the neighborhood closing in on them. Resembling the ever-changing cycle of life, the degeneration that the Collyer brothers experienced manifested itself in the beauty and trash that was stashed in their hoard. Holding onto something beautiful and fearing it would be taken from them, they became neurotic in their efforts to cling to it. The symbolism of trying to hold onto their beautiful past and fear of losing it created the prison they resided in.

Andy Warhol's personal myth and symbolism seemed to live through his notion that everything was art and everything was important; nothing was too small or insignificant. He wanted to be important, a living artwork, and he projected that into his hoard. The items hoarded, from his personal medications and prescriptions to his collection of fan mail, symbolize the ego in crisis seeking a literal way to identify itself.

Ida Mayfield's personal myth was told through her identification with particular objects stored in her trunks due to a fragmented and incomplete process of healthy mourning, which became an autonomous force bigger than oneself. Her hoarding experience was a direct reflection of her unconscious conflict over her shameful identity, repressed into repetitive behaviors of acquiring money and jewelry, which she adopted as her identity. Attempting to avoid her fears, she built her hoard, which symbolically created feelings of safety, identity, and opportunity.

The individuals' personal symbolism for their objects was illuminated through the telling of their myths. Each one had unique symbolic meanings that needed individual interpretation; therefore, a prescribed treatment regimen would foreclose on the symbolic function and deny access to the dynamism of the unconscious.

The next step in the relationship between object and person is to acknowledge the importance of shame in the hoarding condition. Feelings of shame have a direct correlation to feelings of rejection, which can then create awkwardness, uncertainty, self-consciousness, and inhibition. Jacoby (1991) stated, "Shame resides on the borderline between self and other. It plays a critical role in the mediation of interpersonal closeness and distance, sensitively gauging my feelings about how close I can and want to let someone come" (p. 22). The experience of shame, inter-twined with memory, particularly memories of loss, was one of the most important themes shared in all six stories. They all suffered from self-image and self-worth deficiencies, which encouraged them to become dependent on the objects that they believed represented them. The objects in their hoards mirrored what cluttered them on the inside, including both psyche and self. The telling of their stories revealed that each historical figure possessed psychic clutter and residue from unresolved shadow material, which was found in physical form in the piles of trash, stink of rotting food, and dilapidated homes.

Tarrant (1998) stated that a hoarder's setting and objects become his or her *prima materia*, the "gross aspects of life—unrefined, unredeemed by any admixture of spirit and yet a kind of foundation for all that follows, for all wisdom and art" (p. 68). This could be seen in the Beales' rotting house and piles of empty cat food tins, the Collyer brothers' rotting house and dusty contents, Ida's moldy and yellowed money and coins, and Andy's rotting food stored in boxes. Each one of them told stories of a shame-based life: Andy and Edie's self-confidence issues, Andy and Ida's embarrassment about their families of origin, Edith's divorce and being left for Phelan's young secretary, Homer's blindness and the brothers being ridiculed by their Harlem neighbors. These embodied experiences for all six figures gave form to the deeper meaning in their lives, dismembering ego consciousness and facilitating the acquisition of objects to create a perceived veil of protection from all angles.

Although the correlations among loss, attachment, and the hoarding experiences of the individuals studied seem comprehensible, it is not enough for the soul's well-being to discuss the role of loss and hoarding this way. The foundational task of the book was to provide a deeper meaning to each one of their experiences by dropping all plans and duties to treat and cure and instead employing the luminosity that arose out of their complexes to connect to psyche. Max Paxton (2011) stated that many hoarders have suffered failed relationships or the death of someone significant to them (p. 45). Again, this seemed to be a central theme for all historical figures presented in the study. Edith Beale experienced a painful divorce; Edie's relationship with Julius Krug ended painfully and then she experienced the death of her father. Andy lost his father to death at a young age and suffered numerous failed relationships with men. The Collyer brothers lost both parents in their 20s, and Ida suffered the deaths of young siblings, both her parents, and at the end both of her sisters. All six individuals were robbed of loved ones, which conceivably created a need for them to create defenses to hold on tighter to their things.

The final element of the depth psychological approach is commencing the work with soul and psyche in mind. Examining the hoarding condition on a surface level, treating just the compulsion and anxiety, can fall victim to normativism when we seek to understand the condition from the ego function. When each historical figure's story was given a voice, psyche and soul were heard through the hoard, saying that losing parts of themselves and their identity was at stake if they were separated from their objects. It was vital for this book to pay attention to the nuances of each experience in the psyche, without reducing them to some formula of understanding, in order to endure the heat of the opposites: shame and loss. The book's commitment to the depth psychological approach confirmed that the psychological treatment modality endangers people who hoard when it tries to force normative ideas onto their lives and their illness.

All of the six individuals studied possessed hoarding behaviors specific to their experiences, where something else became their source of happiness, identity, and value and they were at the mercy of the fantasy they created. This book has imagined it as the consummation of lovers, a coming together of emotions and physical connectedness between object and person that ruptures the claims made by clinical literature and ego consciousness on behalf of the imaginal and the metaphors and images themselves.

When the depth angle was employed, it allowed the historical figures' unconscious conflicts to surface into consciousness by providing a voice for each historical figure to tell his or her story and uncovering the core schemas that kept each figure stuck in hoarding behaviors. Thomas Moore (2000), in his book *Original Self*, describes the underlying challenge of life and the journey of this research: "When we live from a deeper place, we become palpably aware that life is fundamentally mysterious and is ultimately incomprehensible to our rational ways of thinking" (p. 60). In order to live from a deeper place, it is essential to journey into the unconscious. Since the unconscious cannot be studied directly, one must examine areas that bridge the conscious with the unconscious through a depth psychological lens.

This book explored the unconscious complexes and triggers that keep hoarders stuck in a debilitating condition, and illuminated the connection between identity, value, and the items individuals hoard. Shifting away from the clinical model of "treatment" and "cure" invites in the repressed, forgotten, and denied aspects of self and soul. The further exploration of these shadow sides with individuals who hoard will facilitate healing as well as a deeper understanding of their behaviors. The insight and vivacity that depth psychology offers the therapeutic vocation were illustrated as well.

The clinical literature on the condition of hoarding is abundant, and with the increased pressure for mental health practitioners to provide quick cognitive behavioral interventions, this book invites contemplation of therapeutic opportunities that value the voice of psyche and soul in creating a life of meaning for individuals who hoard. It contributes to the existing literature and advances knowledge in the field of hoarding behaviors by presenting a different and new perspective through the use of a depth psychological lens. This book posed the question: What does soul want in this cluttered and murky setting? The answer is simple: it seeks a qualitative descriptive answer to this question based on a set of core concepts from depth psychology. Soul, spirit, and psyche are all dimensions served by employing a depth approach to the condition of hoarding.

There was an intention throughout the book to bring reflection and insight to describing the personal deep suffering of people who struggle to make sense of their hoarding tendencies. A moment of reflection is sought to see how the work was served by soul. The images of the hoard, setting, and lived experiences of each historical figure individuated from the confines of the repressed shadow and were expressed on a deeper level; this is when soul and psyche were served. As Robert Johnson (1991) concludes, "If you can touch your shadow—within form—and do something out of your ordinary pattern, a great deal of energy will flow from it" (p. 47). That said, objects appear to draw hoarders into the experience of soul-making through excessive acquisition, enlightening their psychological lives and allowing for the transformation of their conscious personalities.

Hollis (1998) notes that people fear loneliness and this keeps them from the essential meeting with themselves; therefore, they will hold tight to terrible relationships rather than risk the fear of letting go of the Other (p. 103). He continues by saying that if we fear loneliness and silence, we cannot be present to ourselves, because companionship with oneself is gained when the silence speaks. Hoarders' clutter keeps them cut off from an authentic relationship with themselves, filling their lives with dazzling objects to distract them from their inner pain and suffering. I concur with Hollis's statement that all relationships are symptomatic of the condition of our inner lives, even our relationships with objects and clutter. No relationship can be any better than our relationship to our own unconscious (Hollis, 1998, p. 47).

A final thought: the journey with these six individuals has brought together deep and moving stories, interwoven like roots of a tree, connected at the deepest level of psyche. We become part of a relationship and a shared collective story and history through the timeless nature of each of our stories. If we understand how we are connected to self, other, and the collective and see our lives interwoven through time and space, it is plausible to view our lives as having a purposeful connection.

REFERENCES

Aaronson, D. (2004). *Andy Warhol: 365 takes*. New York: Abrams.

A+E Television Networks (2013a). Andy Warhol. *Biography.com*. Retrieved from www.biography.com/people/andy-warhol-9523875

A+E Television Networks (2013b). Edith Bouvier Beale. *Biography.com*. Retrieved from www.biography.com/people/edith-bouvier-beale-435518

A+E Television Networks (2013c). Edith Ewing Beale. *Biography.com*. Retrieved from www.biography.com/people/edith-ewing-beale-435560

Abbott, K. (2013). Past imperfect: Everything was fake but her wealth. *Smithsonian.com*. Retrieved from http://blogs.smithsonianmag.com/history/2013/01/everything-was-fake-but-her-wealth/

After fortune (1931, October 26). *Time, 18*(17), 44.

Aged recluse, once belle, has $5,000,000 cash in skirt (1931, October 10). *The Washington Post*, p. 1.

Alexander, I. (1990). *Personology*. London: Duke University Press.

AllPsych Online (2011). *Personality synopsis: Chapter 7: Trait theory—psychogenic needs*. Retrieved from http://allpsych.com/personalitysynopsis/murray.html

Amazing stories (n.d.). Retrieved from http://yoyo.cc.monash.edu.au/~jonno/story5.htm

American Psychiatric Association (1994). *Diagnostic and statistical manual of mental disorders* (4th edn). Washington, DC: Author.

American Psychiatric Association (2013). *Diagnostic and statistical manual of mental disorders* (5th edn). Washington, DC. Author.

Andy Warhol Biography (n.d.). *IMDb.com*. Retrieved from www.imdb.com/name/nm0912238/bio

Andy Warhol Foundation for the Visual Arts. (n.d.). *Andy Warhol biography: Pop artist and cultural icon*. Retrieved from www.warholfoundation.org/legacy/biography.html

Ask.com (n.d.). *Collyer brothers*. Retrieved from www.ask.com/wiki/Collyer_brothers

Au, W., & Cannon, N. (1995). *Urgings of the heart*. New York: Paulist Press.

Bachelard, G. (2002). *Earth and reveries of will* (K. Haltman, Trans). Dallas, TX: Dallas Institute. (Original work published 1948).

Beale, E. B. (2010). *I only mark the hours that shine: Little Edie's diary—1929*. Mill Valley, CA: Grey Gardens Collections.

Beale, E. M. (2009). *Edith Bouvier Beale of Grey Gardens: A life in pictures.* East Hampton, NY: Verlhac.

Bond, D. S. (1993). *Living myth: Personal meaning as a way of life.* Boston, MA: Shambhala.

Bowlby, J. (1980). *Attachment and loss: Vol. 3. Loss: Sadness and depression.* New York: Basic Books.

Bryk, W. (1999). The Collyer brothers of Harlem. *NYPress.com.* Retrieved from http://nypress.com/the-collyer-brothers-of-harlem/

Burns, R. (Director) (2006). *Andy Warhol: A documentary* [Motion picture]. United States: Steeplechase Films.

Cambray, J. (2009, March). *Emergent phenomena and psychotherapy.* Unpublished lecture, Carpinteria, CA: Pacifica Graduate Institute.

Campbell, J. (1988). *The power of myth.* New York: MJF Books.

Carotenuto, A. (1989). *Eros and pathos: Shades of love and suffering.* Toronto, ON: Inner City Books.

Chan, M., Severson, D., & Kelly, M. (Producers) (2009). *Hoarders* [Television series]. New York: A&E Networks.

Clutter [Def. 2] (n.d.). *Merriam-Webster Online.* Retrieved from www.merriam-webster.com/dictionary/clutter

Coppin, J., & Nelson, E. (2005). *The art of inquiry.* Putnam, CT: Spring.

Cox, J. (1964). *The recluse of Herald Square.* Fakenham, Norfolk, England: Cox & Wyman.

Dirda, M. (2009, September 03). The Collyer brothers: A collective obsession. *Washington Post,* p. 26. Retrieved from http://articles.washingtonpost.com/2009-09-03/news/36878997_1_collyers-homer-and-langley-rare-books

Doctorow, E. L. (2009). *Homer and Langley: A novel.* New York: Random House.

Douglas, M. (1966). *Purity and danger.* New York: Routledge.

Ebert, R. (2001, May 11). *The Gleaners and I.* Retrieved from www.rogerebert.com/reviews/the-gleaners-and-i-2001

Edinger, E. F. (1985). *Anatomy of the psyche: Alchemical symbolism in psychotherapy.* Chicago, IL: Open Court Trade and Academic Books.

Epstein, M. (1998*). Going to pieces without falling apart: A Buddhist perspective on wholeness.* New York: Bantam Doubleday Dell.

Ferrell, J. (2006). *Empire of scrounge.* New York: New York University Press.

Frederick, C. (1929). *Selling Mrs. Consumer.* New York: The Business Bourse.

Frost, R., & Hartl, T. (1996). A cognitive behavioral model of compulsive hoarding. *Behaviour Research and Therapy, 34,* 341–350.

Frost, R., & Steketee, G. (2010). *Stuff: Compulsive hoarding and the meaning of things.* New York: Houghton Mifflin Harcourt.

Frost, R., Kyrios, M., McCarthy, K., & Matthews, Y. (2007). Self-ambivalence and attachment to possessions. *Journal of Cognitive Psychotherapy, 21*(3), 232–242.

Frost, R., Steketee, G., Tolin, D., & Renaud, S. (2008). Development and validation of the Clutter Image Rating. *Journal of Psychopathology Behavioral Assessment, 30,* 193–203.

Frost, R., Tolin, D., Steketee, F. K., & Selbo-Bruns, A. (2009). Excessive acquisition in hoarding. *Journal of Anxiety Disorders, 23*(5), 632–639.

Gadamer, H. (1975). *Truth and method.* New York: Continuum.

Gilbert, P., & Andrews, B. (1998). *Shame: Interpersonal behavior, psychopathology, and culture.* New York: Oxford University Press.

Gilliam, C., & Tolin, D. (2010). Compulsive hoarding. *Bulletin of the Menninger Clinic, 74*(2), 93–121.

Giroux, H. (2014). *The violence of organized forgetting: Thinking beyond America's disimagination machine.* San Francisco, CA: City Lights Books.

Goodchild, V. (2001). *Eros and chaos*. York Beach, ME: Nicolas-Hays.

Gray, C. (2002). *What did the Collyer brothers ever do for Harlem?* Retrieved from http://theendofcollection.wordpress.com/category/collyer-brothers/

Greenberg, J., & Jordan, S. (2004). *Andy Warhol: Prince of pop*. New York: Delacorte Press.

Grey Gardens Online (2009). Retrieved from www.greygardensonline.com/

Gutis, P. (1987, July 11). Trash barge to end trip in Brooklyn. *New York Times*. Retrieved from www.nytimes.com/1987/07/11/nyregion/trash-barge-to-end-trip-in-brooklyn.html

Hackett, P. (1989). *The Andy Warhol diaries*. New York: Warner.

Hackett, P., & Warhol, A. (1988). *Andy Warhol's party book*. New York: Crown.

Hannon, J. (2008, Winter). Another look: Andy Warhol's time capsules. *Carnegie Magazine*. Retrieved from www.carnegiemuseums.org/cmag/article.php?id=125

Herring, S. (2011). Collyer curiosa: A brief history of hoarding. *Criticism, 53*(2), 159–188.

Hibernian chronicle: The Mayfield mystery solved (2011, February 17). *The Irish Echo*. Retrieved from http://irishecho.com/2011/02/hibernian-chronicle-the-mayfield-mystery-solved-2/

Hillman, J. (1975). *Re-visioning psychology*. New York: Harper & Row.

Hillman, J. (1981). *The thought of the heart and the soul of the world*. Dallas, TX: Spring.

Hillman, J. (1983a). *Archetypal psychology*. Dallas, TX: Spring.

Hillman, J. (1983b). *Healing fiction*. Woodstock, CT: Spring.

Hillman, J. (1999). *The force of character and the lasting life*. New York: Random House.

Hoard [Def. 1] (n.d.). *Oxford English Dictionary*. Retrieved from www.oxforddictionaries.com/definition/english/hoard

Hollis, J. (1993). *The middle passages: From misery to meaning in middle life*. Toronto, ON: Inner City Books.

Hollis, J. (1996). *Swamplands of the soul: New life in dismal places*. Toronto, ON: Inner City Books.

Hollis, J. (1998). *The Eden project: In search of the magical other*. Toronto, ON: Inner City Books.

Ida Wood's early life is revealed (1937, September 16). *The Hartford Courant*, p. 8.

Jacobi, J. (1959). *Complex/archetype/symbol*. New York: Bollingen Foundation.

Jacoby, M. (1991). *Shame and the origins of self-esteem: A Jungian approach*. New York: Routledge.

Johnson, R. (1991). *Owning your own shadow*. San Francisco, CA: HarperCollins.

Jung, C. (1960, March 25). Letter in English dated March 25, 1960. In *Letters* (Vol. 2, p. 545). Princeton, NJ: Princeton University Press.

Jung, C. (1960). On the nature of the psyche. In R. F. C. Hull (Trans.), *The collected works of C. G. Jung*: (Vol. 8). Princeton, NJ: Bollingen.

Jung, C. (1964). *Man and his symbols*. New York: Dell.

Jung, C. (1973). Preface (R. F. C. Hull, Trans.). In E. Neumann, *Depth psychology and a new ethic* (p. 16). New York: Harper and Row.

Jung, C. (1984) [1938]. *Dream analysis: Notes of the seminar given 1928–1930*. London: Routledge.

Kalsched, D. (1996). *The inner world of trauma*. New York: Routledge.

Keene, A. (2013). Unwrapping Warhol: 572nd time capsule opened. *The Duquesne Duke*. Retrieved from www.theduquesneduke.com/unwrapping-warhol-572nd-time-capsule-opened-1.2972825?pagereq=2#.UpUBBShVjoA

Keith York City (2012). *Homer and Langley Collyer: Hoarders in Harlem*. Retrieved from http://keithyorkcity.wordpress.com/2012/09/28/homer-langley-collyer-hoarders-in-harlem/

Kiedrowski, T. (2011). *Andy Warhol's New York City: Four walks, uptown to downtown.* New York: The Little Bookroom.

Lepselter, S. (2011). The disorder of things: Hoarding narratives in popular media. *Anthropological Quarterly, 84*(4), 919–948.

Lewis, M. (1992). *Shame: The exposed self.* New York: The Free Press.

Lidz, F. (2003a). *Ghosty men: The strange but true story of the Collyer brothers, New York's greatest hoarders.* Bloomsbury, NY: Holtzbrinck.

Lidz, F. (2003b, October 26). The paper chase. *New York Times*, pp. 1–5. Retrieved from www.nytimes.com/2003/10/26/nyregion/the-paper-chase.html?pagewanted=all&src=pm

Lynd, H. (1961). *On shame and the search for identity.* New York: Routledge.

McKnaught, E. (1932, November 27). Boston relatives of woman who hid money in her skirt. *Boston Globe*, p. A54.

Mcqueeney, K. (2012). The ultimate hoarders: Extraordinary story of the two reclusive brothers found dead side-by-side under tons of junk in New York mansion in 1947. *Mail Online.* Retrieved from www.dailymail.co.uk/news/article-2217953/Homer-Langley-Collyer-Hoarder-brothers-killed-clutter-New-York-mansion.html

Maddi, S., & Costa, P. (1972). *Humanism in personology.* Chicago, IL: Aldine-Atherton.

Maier, T. (2004). On phenomenology and classification of hoarding: A review. *Acta Psychiatrica Scandinavica, 110*(5), 323–337.

Mataix-Cols, D., Frost, R., Pertusa, A., Clark, L., Saxena, S., Leckman, J., Stein, J., Hisato, M. D., Matsunga, M. D., & Wilhelm, S. (2010). Hoarding disorder: A new diagnosis for DSM-V? *Depression and Anxiety, 27*, 556–572.

Maysles, A. (n.d.). Albert Maysles on "Grey Gardens." *Buffalo Magazine.* Retrieved from http://buffalozine.com/film/albert-maysles-grey-gardens

Maysles, A. (Director) (2006). *The Beales of Grey Gardens* [DVD]. United States: The Criterion Collection.

Moore, T. (2000*). Original self.* New York: HarperCollins.

Morrison, A. (1998). *The culture of shame.* Northvale, NJ: Jason Aronson.

Mrs Ida Wood, rich hermit dies (1937, February 28). *Boston Globe*, p. A9.

Muchnic, S. (1988). Rummaging through the Andy Warhol estate. *Los Angeles Times.* Retrieved from http://articles.latimes.com/1988–02–21/entertainment/ca-44010_1_andy-warhol-estate/2

Murray, H. (1981). *Endeavors in psychology: Selections from the personology of Henry A. Murray.* New York: Harper & Row.

Nedelisky, A., & Steele, M. (2009). Attachment to people and to objects in obsessive compulsive disorder: An exploratory comparison of hoarders and non-hoarders. *Attachment & Human Development, 11*(4), 365–383.

Ober, L. (2013). Dead bees, nail clippings, and priceless art in Warhol's "time capsules." *NPR.* Retrieved from www.npr.org/2013/11/02/242174661/dead-bees-nail-clippings-and-priceless-art-in-warhols-time-capsules

Packard, V. (1960). *The waste makers.* New York: David McKay Co.

Palmer, R. (1969). *Hermeneutics.* Evanston, IL: Northwestern University Press.

Paxton, M. (2011). *The secret lives of hoarders.* New York: Penguin Group.

Penzel, F. (2011). Langley Collyer: The mystery hoarder of Harlem. *Western Suffolk Psychological Services.* Retrieved from www.wsps.info/index.php?option=com_content&view=article&id=72:langley-collyer-the-mystery-hoarder-of-harlem&catid=0:

Perborg, B. (n.d.). *The Collyer brothers: Recluses in New York City.* Retrieved from www.bjornperborg.com/pages/samlarnabox006en.html

Pertusa, A., Fullana, M., Singh, S., Alonso, P., Menchon, J., & Mataix-Cols, D. (2008). Compulsive hoarding: OCD symptoms, distinct clinical syndrome or both? *American Medical Journal of Psychiatry, 165*, 1289–1298.

Pertusa, A., Frost, R. O., Fullana, M. A., Samuels, J., Steketee, G., Tolin, D., Saxena, S., Leckman, J., & Mataix-Cols, D. (2010). Refining the boundaries of compulsive hoarding: A review. *Clinical Psychology Review, 30*, 371–386

Pilkington, E. (2007, December 5). Warhol's weird world. *The Guardian.* Retrieved from www.the guardian.com/artanddesign/2007/dec/05/art

Plushnick-Masti, R. (2009). What's not inside Warhol "time capsules"? *Boston.com.* Retrieved from www.boston.com/ae/theater_arts/articles/2009/09/01/whats_inside_andy_warhols_time_capsules_you_name_it/

Pritchett, L. (2009). *Going green.* Norman, OK: University of Oklahoma Press.

Rich recluse had hobby for market (1931, November 8). *Boston Globe,* p. A44.

Romanyshyn, R. (1999). *The soul in grief.* Berkeley, CA: North Atlantic Books.

Romanyshyn, R. (2002). *Ways of the heart.* Pittsburgh, PA: Trivium.

Schlitz, M., Amoorok, T., & Micozzi, M. (2005). *Consciousness and healing: Integral approaches to mind-body medicine.* Philadelphia, PA: Elsevier.

Serendipity 3 (n.d.). *History.* Retrieved from www.serendipity3.com/history.htm

Sheehy, G. (1972, January). The secret of Grey Gardens. *New York.* Retrieved from http://nymag.com/news/features/56102/index2.html

Sheehy, G. (2014). *Daring: My passages.* New York: HarperCollins.

Slattery, D. (2002). A riff on the richness of reverie. In Gaston Bachelard (Trans.), *Earth and reveries of will: An essay on the imagination of matter* (p. 4). Dallas, TX: Dallas Institute.

Sooke, A. (2007). Lifting the lid on Warhol's time capsules. *The Telegraph.* Retrieved from www.telegraph.co.uk/culture/art/3666842/Lifting-the-lid-on-Warhols-Time-Capsules.html

Steer, D. (2003). *Dr. Ernest Drake's dragonology: The complete book of dragons.* Cambridge, MA: Candlewick Press.

Stein, M. (1998). *Jung's map of the soul.* Peru, IL: Carus.

Steketee, G., Frost, R., & Kyrios, M. (2003). Cognitive aspects of compulsive hoarding. *Cognitive Therapy and Research, 27*, 467–479.

Strasser, S. (1999). *Waste and want.* New York: Henry Holt & Co.

Sucsy, M. (Director) (2009). *Grey Gardens* [DVD]. United States: HBO Films.

Tarrant, J. (1998). *The light inside the dark.* New York: HarperCollins.

The strange story of the recluse of Herald Square (2013, January 9). *Ephemeral New York.* Retrieved from http://ephemeralnewyork.wordpress.com/2013/01/09/the-story-behind-the-recluse-of-herald-square

Tolin, D., Frost, R., & Steketee, G. (2007). *Buried in treasures: Help for compulsive acquiring, saving, and hoarding.* New York: Oxford University Press.

Tolin, D., Frost, R., Steketee, G., & Fitch, K. (2008). Family burden of compulsive hoarding. Results of an Internet survey. *Behavior Research and Therapy, 46*, 334–344.

Tolin, D., Meunier, S., Frost, R., & Steketee, G. (2010). Course of compulsive hoarding and its relationship to life events. *Journal of Depression & Anxiety, 27*, 829–838.

Tremayne, C., Poertner, M., & Wolfe, M. (Producers) (2010). *American Pickers* [Television series]. New York: A&E Networks.

Von Franz, M. (1980). *Alchemy.* Toronto, ON: Inner City Books.

Von Franz, M. (1988). *Psyche and matter.* Boston, MA: Shambhala.

Walker, S. (2002). *Jung and the Jungians on myth.* New York: Routledge.

Warhol, A. (1975). *The philosophy of Andy Warhol.* New York: Harcourt Brace Jovanovich.

Webb, J. (2009). A pictorial history of Grey Gardens. *Cote de Texas*. Retrieved from http://cotedetexas.blogspot.com/2009/05/pictorial-history-of-grey-gardens.html

Weiss, K. (2010). Hoarding, hermitage, and the law: Why we love the Collyer brothers. *Journal of the American Academy of Psychiatry and the Law Online, 38*(2), 251–257.

Wikipedia (2014a). *American pickers.* Retrieved from http://en.wikipedia.org/wiki/American_Pickers

Wikipedia (2014b). *Hoarders.* Retrieved from http://en.wikipedia.org/wiki/Hoarders

Wikipedia (2014c). *Hoarding.* Retrieved from http://en.wikipedia.org/wiki/Hoarding

Wikman, M. (2004). *Pregnant darkness: Alchemy and the rebirth of consciousness.* Berwick, ME: Nicolas-Hays.

Wilson, J. (2002). *Trash and treasure: Senses of cinema.* Retrieved from http://sensesofcinema.com/2002/feature-articles/gleaners/

Winnicott, D. (1971). The location of cultural experience. In *Playing and reality* (pp. 35, 100). New York: Basic Books.

Wood, C. (2010, October 15). My crazy aunt Ida. *Personal Liberty Digest.* Retrieved from http://personalliberty.com/2010/10/15/my-crazy-aunt-ida/

Woodman, M., & Dickson, E. (1996). *Dancing in the flames: The dark goddess in the transformation of consciousness.* Boston, MA: Shambhala.

Worden, H. (1953). *Out of this world.* Toronto, ON: Thomas Allen.

Workman, C. (Director) (1990). *Superstar: The life and times of Andy Warhol* [Motion picture]. New York: Marilyn Lewis Entertainment.

Wrbican, M. (2007, November 19). Archivist Matt Wrbican reveals the weird and wonderful contents of the artist's "time capsules." *The Sydney Morning Herald.* Retrieved from www.smh.com.au/news/arts/warhols-hoard-a-treasure-trove/2007/11/19/1195321691266.html

Wright, L. (1978). *My life at Grey Gardens: 13 months and beyond: A true and factual book.* East Hampton, NY: Author.

Wright, R. (1930, August). The decay of tinkers recalls olden days of repairing. *House & Garden, 48.*

INDEX

Herald Square Hotel 96–100; hidden
fortune 98–99; living space usage 118;
loss 106, 114; marriage 92–95; new
identity 93–94; object clusters 109; pain
avoidance 118; personal myth 119–120;
President Lincoln 94–95; shadows in
settings 110; shame 107–108, 114;
sisters, death of 96; squalor of rooms
98–100; stock market hobby 95
Wood, Mary 91, 93, 96, 99, 100, 102
Wood, Otis 97
Worden, Helen 73, 74, 76, 78, 79–80
Wrbican, Matt 89–90
Wright, Lois 63–67

55706640R00084

Made in the USA
San Bernardino, CA
04 November 2017